THE ULTIMATE FUNCTIONAL
LEVEL 1 LEARN AND P

FUNKY SKILLS FUN

FUNCTIONAL SKILLS ENGLISH LEVEL 1

BY

PAUL MEADE

LEARN ENGLISH WHILE YOU PLAY

The Ultimate Functional Skills English Level 1 Learn and Play Book

ISBN: 9781804677766
Perfect Bound

First published in 2023 by bookvault Publishing, Peterborough, United Kingdom

An Environmentally friendly book printed and bound in England by bookvault, powered by printondemand-worldwide

THE MENU OF FUN

PUNCTUATION

Full Stop or Period (●) - is used to indicate the end of a sentence or a statement. It is also used in abbreviations. Example: "I went to the shops."

Comma (,) - is used to separate items in a list, provide pauses in a sentence, or separate clauses. Example: "I need to buy apples, oranges, and bananas."

Question mark (?) - is used at the end of a sentence to indicate a direct question. Example: "What time is the meeting?"

Exclamation mark (!) - is used to indicate strong emotions, suprise, or emphasis.
Example: "That's amazing!"

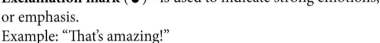

Quotation marks (" ") - are used to enclose direct speech, dialogue, or a quote from someone. Example: She said, "Hello, how are you?"

Colon (:) - is used to introduce a list, an explanation, or a quotation. Example: "I have three favourite colours: blue, green, and purple."

Semicolon (;) - is used to connect two closely related independent clauses or to separate items in a list when those items already contain commas. Example: "I have to finish my work; then I can go home."

Dash (——) - is used to indicate a break or interruption in a sentence or to emphasize a particular point. Example: "She loved two things—traveling and reading."

Parentheses or brackets ( ) - are used to enclose additional information or explanations that are not crucial to the main sentence. Example: "The event (which was held outdoors) was a great success."

Ellipsis (● ● ●) - is used to indicate the omission of words, a pause, or trailing off in thought. Example: "I don't know... it's just..."

Hyphen (‐) - is used to join words together or to indicate a word break at the end of a line. Example: "Well-being" or "twenty-one."

Apostrophe (ʹ) - is used to **indicate possession** or to **form contractions**. Example: "John's car" or "can't" (instead of "cannot").

Punctuation Level 1 Apostrophe Contraction

Fill in the crossword using an apostrophe where necessary.

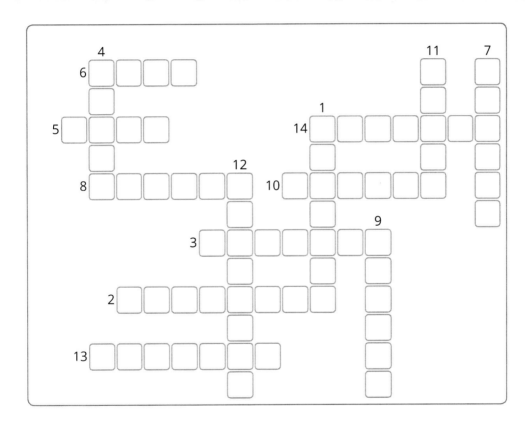

Across
2. should not (9)
3. could not (8)
5. is not (5)
6. will not (5)
8. there is (7)
10. must not (7)
13. could have (8)
14. would have (8)

Down
1. would not (8)
4. was not (6)
7. does not (7)
9. they are (7)
11. did not (6)
12. should have (9)

Punctuation Level 1 Possessive Apostrophe

💡 How do you show that the subject owns something - Possessive Apostrophe

1.

Oliver | cat

A ☐ Oliver's cat   B ☐ Oliver' cat

C ☐ Olivers' cat   D ☐ The cat of Oliver

2.

the girls | bags

A ☐ the girl's bag   B ☐ the girls' bags

C ☐ the girl's bags   D ☐ The bags of the girls

3.

Luigi | bus

A ☐ Luigis' bus   B ☐ Luigi bus

C ☐ Luigi's bus   D ☐ The bus of luigi

4.

the boys | books

A ☐ the boys' books

B ☐ the boy's book

C ☐ the boy's books

D ☐ The books of the boys

5.

Mr Brown | hat

A ☐ Mr Browns hat   B ☐ Mr Brown's hat

C ☐ Mr Browns' hat   D ☐ The hat of Mr Brown

6.

Rose | bike

A ☐ Rosys' bike   B ☐ Rosy' bike

C ☐ Rosy's bike   D ☐ The bike of Rosy

7.

A ☐ the twin's hats   B ☐ the twins' hats

C ☐ the twin hats   D ☐ the hats of the twins

8

Punctuation Level 1 Quiz 1

💡 Identify the Punctuation Marks.

1.

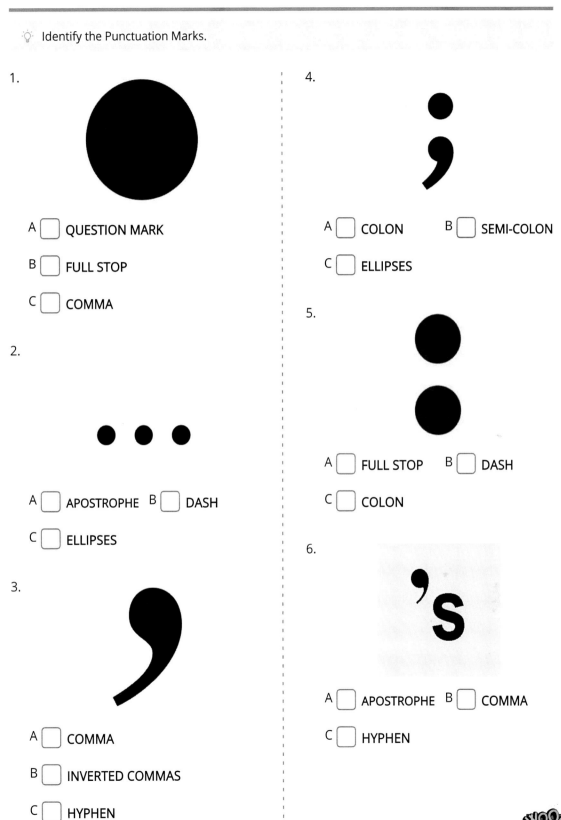

A ☐ QUESTION MARK

B ☐ FULL STOP

C ☐ COMMA

2.

A ☐ APOSTROPHE   B ☐ DASH

C ☐ ELLIPSES

3.

A ☐ COMMA

B ☐ INVERTED COMMAS

C ☐ HYPHEN

4.

A ☐ COLON   B ☐ SEMI-COLON

C ☐ ELLIPSES

5.

A ☐ FULL STOP   B ☐ DASH

C ☐ COLON

6.

A ☐ APOSTROPHE   B ☐ COMMA

C ☐ HYPHEN

7.

A ☐ QUESTION MARK

B ☐ HYPHEN

C ☐ DASH

8.

A ☐ INVERTED COMMAS

B ☐ COMMA

C ☐ QUESTION MARK

9.

A ☐ EXCLAMATION MARK

B ☐ FULL STOP

C ☐ QUESTION MARK

10.

A ☐ SEMI-COLON

B ☐ EXCLAMATION MARK

C ☐ APOSTROPHE

11.

A ☐ BRACKETS   B ☐ ELLIPSES

C ☐ COLON

12.

A ☐ HYPHEN   B ☐ DASH

C ☐ FULL STOP

Punctuation Level 1 Quiz 2

💡 How do you use Punctuation?

1. what do you use before but and because?

A ☐ apostrophe B ☐ full stop

C ☐ comma D ☐ question mark

2. when do you use an apostrophe?

A ☐ ending a sentence

B ☐ replacing a conjunction

C ☐ sentence starters

D ☐ replacing a letter (don't can't)

3. what do you use a semicolon for?

A ☐ replacing a conjunction

B ☐ starting a list

C ☐ starting or ending speech

D ☐ separating a sentence

4. what do you put when you start a list?

A ☐ apostrophe B ☐ colon

C ☐ semicolon D ☐ comma

5. what do you use a question mark for?

A ☐ being angry at someone B ☐ asking a question

C ☐ replacing a conjunction D ☐ starting a list

6. when do you use an exclamation mark?

A ☐ separating a sentence

B ☐ ending a sentence

C ☐ when you are yelling at someone

D ☐ replacing a conjunction

7. what do you put at the end of a sentence?

A ☐ comma B ☐ semicolon

C ☐ question mark D ☐ full stop

8. what do you sometimes use at a end of a paragraph?

A ☐ ellipsis B ☐ exclamation mark

C ☐ apostrophe D ☐ colon

9. What do you use to show someone is speaking directly?

A ☐ 66 99 quotation marks

B ☐ ? question mark

C ☐ ! exclamation mark

D ☐ , two commas

10. What should go at the end of this sentence

A ☐ exclamation mark B ☐ full stop

C ☐ question mark D ☐ comma

11. How would you show that I'm shouting a sentence?

A ☐ question mark B ☐ elipses

C ☐ exclamation mark D ☐ full stop

12. What do I use to abbreviate (shorten) the word cannot?

A ☐ comma B ☐ quotation marks

C ☐ apostrophe D ☐ semi colon

13. What do I use before writing a list?

A ☐ semi colon B ☐ colon

C ☐ comma D ☐ full stop

14. Every sentence starts with...

A ☐ a full stop B ☐ a quotation mark

C ☐ a comma D ☐ a capital letter

15. Which of the following needs a capital letter?

A ☐ school B ☐ home

C ☐ paris D ☐ church

16. Which of the following needs a capital letter?

A ☐ st mary's church B ☐ my home

C ☐ my house D ☐ my street

Punctuation Level 1 Quiz 3

Draw a line to match the Punctuation Marks to their definition.

!	Indicates pause in a sentence
" "	Separates two related sentences
;	Indicates direct speech
:	Separates extra information from the main part of the sentence
-	Can be used like a dash to separate extra information from the main point of sentence
.	At the end of a sentence
?	Goes at the end of a question
,	Shows a letter has been left out, or shows possession
( )	Introduces a list
'	Goes at the end of a dramatic sentence or to show surprise

12

Punctuation Level 1 Quiz Airplane

Draw a path from each airplane to its answer - don't crash into other clouds along the way

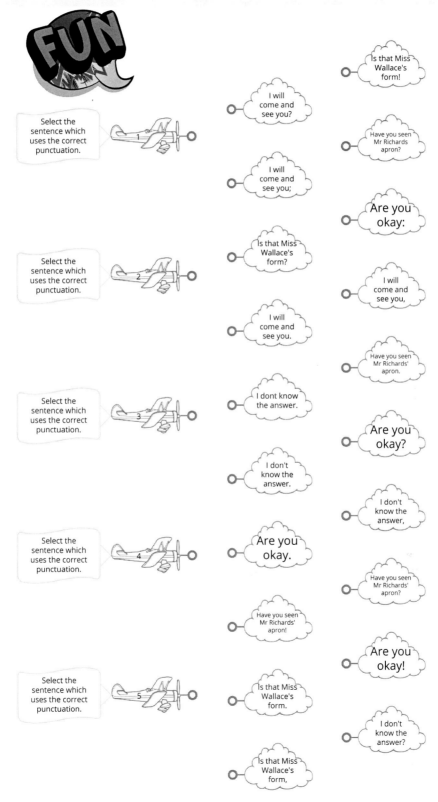

It might seem obvious, but the first thing before you do any form of writing is to identify your audience. Who will read this article, story, email, or press release? The answer to this question may well determine the form. If you need to ask your boss formally for a raise, you probably aren't going to write it in a Press Release. Hopefully, if you can't meet in person, you will send a professional-looking email. Similarly, if you have been put in charge of announcing a community Christmas carol concert, you may well decide to put up a few prominently placed posters, as well as issue a Press Release that might be sent to local and regional newspapers, as well as radio stations. An email is probably not the best method of communicating this event unless you attach a poster to it.

So, who is your audience? Are you aiming your message directly to the reader? For example, by sending an email to your boss, or, are you sending a Press Release to an online or newspaper editor, who you then expect to interpret the information and pass it on in some form, to the readers? In the latter, the information and form you present to the editor, will be different from the information and form you would present to members of the public.

Writing for your readership isn't just about knowing the form, or age demographic, it is about understanding every aspect of your audience. Some considerations are:

AGE
ETHNICITY
CULTURAL SENSITIVITIES
SEXUAL PREFERENCE OR IDENTITY
RELIGIOUS AFFILIATION
DISABILITIES OR SPECIAL NEEDS

The main purposes of a text can vary depending on the context and genre, but everyone writes for a reason; they have a purpose. At Level 1 you may be asked to figure out the purpose.

Informative: The purpose of an informative text is to provide knowledge, facts, or explanations about a particular subject. It aims to educate or enlighten the reader. Examples include news articles, textbooks, and encyclopedias.

Persuasive: Persuasive texts aim to convince or persuade the reader to adopt a certain viewpoint, take specific action, or change their beliefs or behaviors. They often use persuasive techniques, logical arguments, and emotional appeals. Examples include opinion articles, advertisements, and political speeches.

Narrative: Narrative texts tell a story or recount a sequence of events. Their purpose is to entertain the reader through engaging characters, plot development, and descriptive language. Examples include novels, short stories, and memoirs.

Descriptive: Descriptive texts aim to create a vivid sensory experience for the reader by providing detailed descriptions of people, places, objects, or events. Their purpose is to paint a clear picture in the reader's mind. Examples include travel writing, poetry, and product descriptions. "It was a long, narrow road with trees overhanging."

Instructive: Instructive texts provide step-by-step guidance or directions on how to perform a task, operate a device, or complete a process. Their purpose is to inform and enable the reader to follow specific instructions. Examples include manuals, recipes, and tutorials. "Step One. Open the box."

Entertaining: The purpose of entertaining texts is to amuse, engage, or captivate the reader. They focus on providing enjoyment and escapism through humor, imaginative stories, or engaging content. Examples include jokes, comics, and entertaining articles.

It's important to note that texts can often serve multiple purposes simultaneously or have additional purposes specific to their intended audience or context.

At level 1, the following is the kind of text you will get. You need to read it, then answer a series of questions, where **all the answers are found within the text**. Have a go at this example. Please write the answers in the space provided.

Joey eagerly anticipated his visit to the football game on Saturday. The stadium buzzed with excitement as fans filled the stands, donning their team colours. Joey, wearing his favourite team shirt, joined the roar of the crowd, cheering for his beloved team. The game unfolded with exhilarating plays and nail-biting moments. Joey's heart raced as his team scored a last-minute goal, securing a thrilling victory. The stadium erupted in cheers, and Joey couldn't help but join in the jubilation. It was a memorable day filled with unforgettable moments for Joey at the football game.

1. What event did Joey attend on Saturday? ....

2. How did Joey show his support for his team? ....

3. What was the atmosphere like at the stadium? ....

4. What happened during the game that made Joey's heart race? ....

5. How did Joey feel at the end of the game? ....

Read the text, then try and match up what each section is talking about.

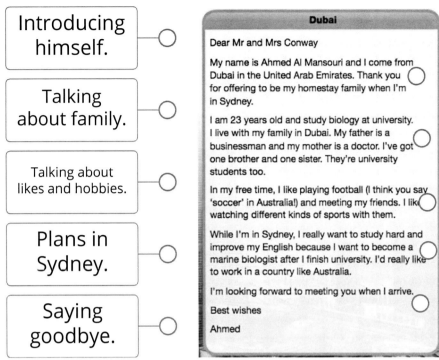

Introducing himself.

Talking about family.

Talking about likes and hobbies.

Plans in Sydney.

Saying goodbye.

Dubai

Dear Mr and Mrs Conway

My name is Ahmed Al Mansouri and I come from Dubai in the United Arab Emirates. Thank you for offering to be my homestay family when I'm in Sydney.

I am 23 years old and study biology at university. I live with my family in Dubai. My father is a businessman and my mother is a doctor. I've got one brother and one sister. They're university students too.

In my free time, I like playing football (I think you say 'soccer' in Australia!) and meeting my friends. I like watching different kinds of sports with them.

While I'm in Sydney, I really want to study hard and improve my English because I want to become a marine biologist after I finish university. I'd really like to work in a country like Australia.

I'm looking forward to meeting you when I arrive.

Best wishes

Ahmed

Carly's Sunday visit to the zoo was a day filled with excitement and wonder. Armed with her camera and a sense of curiosity, she embarked on her animal-filled adventure. As she strolled through the zoo, Carly came face to face with majestic lions, their powerful roars resonating through the air. She marveled at the playful antics of mischievous monkeys, swinging effortlessly from tree branches.

The vibrant colors of tropical birds caught her attention as they soared gracefully overhead. Carly even had the opportunity to feed gentle giraffes, their long necks reaching down to accept the offered treats. It was a day of awe-inspiring encounters and cherished memories at the zoo.

1. Where did Carly visit on Sunday? ....

2. What did Carly bring with her to the zoo? ....

3. Which animals did Carly encounter during her visit? ....

4. How did Carly describe the lions at the zoo? ....

5. What experience did Carly have with the giraffes? ....
....

Purpose of Text Level 1 Quiz 2

💡 What is the main purpose for each of these texts?

1. The main purpose of this text is to :

A ◯ Persuade
B ◯ Inform
C ◯ Describe
D ◯ Instruct

2. The main purpose of this text is to :

A ◯ Instruct
B ◯ Invite
C ◯ Persuade
D ◯ Entertain

3. The main purpose of this text is to :

A ◯ Persuade
B ◯ Inform
C ◯ Instruct
D ◯ Describe

4. The main purpose of this text is to :

A ◯ entertain
B ◯ persuade
C ◯ instruct
D ◯ inform

5. The main purpose of this text is to :

A ◯ Instruct
B ◯ Inform
C ◯ Persuade
D ◯ Entertain

6. The main purpose of this text is to :

A ◯ Instruct
B ◯ Persuade
C ◯ inform
D ◯ entertain

7. The main purpose of this text is to :

A ◯ instruct
B ◯ entertain
C ◯ inform
D ◯ persuade

8. The main purpose of this text is to :

A ◯ persuade
B ◯ inform
C ◯ instruct
D ◯ entertain

9. The main purpose of this text is to :

A ◯ inform
B ◯ persuade
C ◯ instruct
D ◯ describe

10. The main purpose of this text is to :

A ◯ advise
B ◯ persuade
C ◯ entertain
D ◯ inform

Purpose of Text Level 1 Quiz 1

💡 Try and figure out why each text has been written - what is the purpose?

1. What does TAP stand for?

   A ◯ Text type, audience, purpose

   B ◯ Text, advise, purpose

   C ◯ Topic, audience, purpose

2. What different purposes might a text have?

   A ◯ To write, read or study

   B ◯ To persuade, entertain or inform

   C ◯ To write, advise or post on a wall

3. What is the purpose of a concert poster?

   A ◯ To persuade people to attend or to inform people about the event

   B ◯ To persuade people to attend and instruct the reader to book tickets immediately

   C ◯ To persuade people and argue why it would be a great place to go

4. What is the purpose of an in-flight emergency leaflet?

   A ◯ To instruct people of procedures and advise of what to do in an emergency

   B ◯ To persuade people to buy in-flight snacks

   C ◯ To entertain people during the flight

5. How would a charity leaflet differ from an in-flight emergency leaflet?

   A ◯ The charity leaflet would contain more information

   B ◯ The charity leaflet would try to persuade the reader to donate instead of instructing the reader of what to do in an emergency

   C ◯ The in-flight leaflet would be more persuasive than a charity leaflet

6. What is meant when referring to the audience of a text?

   A ◯ The person writing it

   B ◯ The particular group of people that the text was aimed at when written

   C ◯ The people viewing the text if it is displayed

7. What would you need to look for when deciding on the audience of a text?

   A ◯ How much information has been included within the text

   B ◯ How interesting the language is within the text

   C ◯ The layout and language used that might be aimed at a particular age group or experts of a particular topic

8. What contextual information could you look for within the text?

   A ◯ How difficult the words are to read and understand

   B ◯ The topic, the tone used and particular language - Standard English or a particular dialect

   C ◯ The way that it is laid out on the page

9. What would indicate that the audience of the text are children?

   A ◯ An adult was not reading it

   B ◯ A standard font and laid out in paragraphs

   C ◯ Bright colours, simplified language and a fun layout

10. What would indicate that the purpose of the text is to persuade?

   A ◯ Use of persuasive techniques and a clear aim to sell a product, idea or event to the reader

   B ◯ Bright colours and information about the price of a product

   C ◯ A paragraph about the drawbacks of a product and contact details of the company

Purpose of Text Level 1 Quiz 3

Rearrange these letters to spell out the correct Purpose of Text.

1. A leaflet about a theme park

M O R F N I

2. Assembly details for Ikea Furniture

T N S I C R U T

3. An advert in a newspaper

E E R P D U A S

4. A web page telling how to save money

E I S V D A

5. A report giving both sides of an argument

S S D S I U C

6. A letter protesting dog walking on public beaches

U G E R A

7. A recipe for making apple pie

T N S I C R U T

8. If you want to get your point across

U G E R A

9. Trying to get someone to agree with you

E E R P D U A S

10. A notice next to a fire extinguisher

T N S I C R U T

PLEASE NOTE:

ALL ADVERTISING IS TRYING TO PERSUADE.

In Level 1 texts, if it is an advert then the answer is probably going to be Persuade. They are trying to get you to buy something.

The same goes for Charity appeals. They are trying to Persuade you to make a donation, or take in a stray animal. But, they are almost always trying to Persuade.

Purpose of Text Level 1 Quiz 5

💡 Write in the box provided the purpose of each text from the words listed below.

1. Turn left at the end of the road. Go as far as the traffic lights. Turn right.

2. Give water Give lifeGive £2 a month

3. Great news for people aged 50 and over! Low cost Home Insurance

4. This year there has been a lot of flooding due to the high rainfall. Lots of homes were flooded.

5. Your motor insurance is due for renewal

6. Melt the butter and sugarMix in the flourBeat in the eggsAdd to the mixture

7. You can't afford to miss this offer!

8. This garment must be dry cleaned

9. Palace Theatre Monday 13th June 7.30 pmJunior ShowtimeStalls D13

10. The sky was so clear and blue. The wind whistled around my ears.

11. Ten students are in my ESOL class. They are Polish, Romanian, Pakistani and Spanish.

Describe
Persuade
Inform
Instruct

Purpose of Text Level 1 Quiz Airplane

Draw a path from each airplane to its answer - don't crash into other clouds along the way

Leaflet about election	 1		
All about a hotel	 2	INSTRUCT 	PERSUADE 
An advert	 3	ARGUE	DISCUSS 
A letter protesting something	 4	 DESCRIBE	INFORM 
A report about traffic near schools	 5		ADVISE 
A recipe	 6		
Warnings around a swimming pool	 7		

GRAMMAR

Common grammatical errors can vary depending on the specific language and context, but here are some examples of frequent grammatical errors in English:

Improper use of capital letters: Remember that every sentence begins with a capital letter, and that proper nouns (names of places, people and things) should have a capital letter at the beginning. For example: Paris, France   St Michael's Church   Joan Smith

Subject-Verb Agreement: This error occurs when the subject and verb in a sentence do not match in terms of number (singular or plural). Example: "The dog chase the cat." (Incorrect) should be "The dog chases the cat." (Correct)

Misuse of Apostrophes: One common error is using apostrophes incorrectly in possessive forms or contractions. Example: "The cat's are playing in the yard." (Incorrect) should be "The cats are playing in the yard." (Correct)

Run-On Sentences: These occur when multiple independent clauses are incorrectly joined without appropriate punctuation or conjunctions. Example: "I went to the store I bought some groceries." (Incorrect) should be "I went to the store, and I bought some groceries." (Correct)

Sentence Fragments: These are incomplete sentences that lack a subject, verb, or complete thought. Example: "Running in the park on a sunny day." (Incorrect) should be "I enjoy running in the park on a sunny day." (Correct)

Incorrect Word Usage: Using the wrong word or confusing homophones (words that sound alike but have different meanings) can lead to errors. Example: "Their going to the party tonight." (Incorrect) should be "They're going to the party tonight." (Correct)

Lack of Agreement Between Pronouns and Antecedents (the thing that comes before or after): This error occurs when the pronoun does not match in terms of gender, number, or person. Example: "Each student should bring their own textbook." (Incorrect) should be "Each student should bring his or her own textbook." (Correct)

Grammar Level 1 Quiz 1

💡 Look at the Spelling, Punctuation and Grammar before you choose a correct sentence.

1. Which sentence is correct?

   A ☐ Taylors dog's are very noisy.   B ☐ Taylor's dogs are very noisy.

2. Which sentence is correct?

   A ☐ We should have come earlier.   B ☐ We should of come earlier.

3. Which sentence uses Standard English?

   A ☐ We was all really excited about our holiday.

   B ☐ We is all really excited about our holiday.

   C ☐ We are all really excited about our holiday.

4. Which sentence uses Standard English?

   A ☐ I did my homework last night.   B ☐ I done my homework last night.

5. My Auntie Sue lives alone. With this in mind, which sentence is punctuated correctly?

   A ☐ I am going to my aunties house later.   B ☐ I am going to my auntie's house later.

   C ☐ I am going to my aunties' house later.

6. Which sentence has the correct use of inverted commas for direct speech?

   A ☐ "Will you come to my party?" Sophie asked me.

   B ☐ "Will you come to my party"? Sophie asked me.

   C ☐ "Will you come to my party? Sophie asked me."

Grammar Level 1 Quiz 2

💡 Put a check under each mole that should start with a capital letter

cities   animals   names   seasons

road names   birthday   months of the year   personal pronoun 'i'

book titles   plants   days of week   common nouns

adverbs   verbs   rivers and oceans   food

countries   adjectives   PSSST

Grammar Level 1 Quiz 3

💡 Test your Grammar Skills!

1. Which kind of punctuation mark would complete the sentence? Can we go to the cinema please

A ◯ !   B ◯ .

C ◯ ,   D ◯ ?

2. Which word completes the sentence?
We_____our bikes.

A ◯ rided   B ◯ rides

C ◯ riding   D ◯ rode

3. look at the words. Which needs an **es** to make it into a plural?

A ◯ pencil   B ◯ fox

C ◯ dog   D ◯ chair

4. Which sentence is a statement?

A ◯ What time is the bus due to arrive?

B ◯ I rode my bike to school.

C ◯ What an enormous aeroplane!

D ◯ Bring your scooter when you come to play.

5. Which sentence is a command?

A ◯ What time does the pool open?

B ◯ Bring your swimming costume to the pool.

C ◯ What an amazing swim!

D ◯ I am learning to swim.

6. Click on the verb in this sentence. Lottie was jumping really high on the trampoline.

A ◯ trampoline

B ◯ high

C ◯ was

D ◯ really

7. Which sentence is in the past tense?

A ◯ Tom rode his bike.

B ◯ Daniel is running.

C ◯ Rebecca will read her book.

D ◯ Joe is writing.

8. What word is the contracted form of **could have?**

A ◯ could'ave   B ◯ coul've

C ◯ could've   D ◯ could ve

woooooo
25

Grammar Level 1 Quiz 4

💡 Keep on Going! Know your Grammar!

1. Click on the correct word to complete the sentence. **We were_____ on our topics.**

   A ⃝ worked B ⃝ works

   C ⃝ working D ⃝ work

2. Click on the correct word to complete the sentence in the **past tense. I _____to Scotland during the school holidays.**

   A ⃝ go B ⃝ going

   C ⃝ went D ⃝ was

3. Click on the correct word to complete the sentence. **Tomorrow, we could go for a walk _____play games indoors.**

   A ⃝ when B ⃝ or

   C ⃝ because D ⃝ if

4. Click on the correct word to complete the sentence. **_____ you go to the park, you can play a game.**

   A ⃝ And B ⃝ So

   C ⃝ But D ⃝ If

5. Which sentence is a **command**?

   A ⃝ Pack away your paints now.

   B ⃝ You should be proud of your work.

   C ⃝ Will you show me your painting?

   D ⃝ That's your best work yet!

6. Choose the correct suffix to add to the word **fall** in this sentence. **The autumn leaves are fall___ to the ground.**

   A ⃝ ed B ⃝ s

   C ⃝ est D ⃝ ing

7. Choose a suffix to add to the word **fast** in this sentence. **The hare knew that he could run fast___ than the tortoise.**

   A ⃝ er B ⃝ est

   C ⃝ ing D ⃝ ed

8. What type of word is in bold in this sentence? Gran thought the flowers were **pretty.**

   A ⃝ noun B ⃝ verb

   C ⃝ adjective D ⃝ adverb

9. Why do the bold words start with a capital letter? On **Saturday** morning, **Sarah** and her family went on holiday to **Scotland.**

   A ⃝ They are nouns B ⃝ they are proper nouns

   C ⃝ they are adjectives D ⃝ at the beginning of a sentence.

10. How many nouns are in this sentence? **You have left your pencil on the bench over there.**

    A ⃝ 1 B ⃝ 2

    C ⃝ 3 D ⃝ 4

11. What type of sentence is this? **One day, Ali decided to make a toy robot.**

    A ⃝ a question B ⃝ a statement

    C ⃝ a command D ⃝ an exclamation

12. Click on the word which is an adverb in this sentence. **Jamie knocked softly on his brother's bedroom door.**

    A ⃝ knocked B ⃝ door

    C ⃝ softly D ⃝ brother

13. Which sentence uses an apostrophe correctly?

    A ⃝ Lucy's bag is green and has lots of pockets.

    B ⃝ Lucys' bag is green and has lots of pockets.

    C ⃝ Lucys bag is green and has lot's of pockets.

    D ⃝ Lucys bag is green and has lots of pocket's.

14. Which sentence uses a comma correctly?

    A ⃝ The museum shop sell,s posters mugs and badges.

    B ⃝ The museum, shop sells posters mugs an badges.

    C ⃝ The museum shop sells posters mugs, and badges.

    D ⃝ The museum shop sells posters, mugs and badges.

15. Which punctuation mark completes the sentence? **What a wonderful present you gave me**

    A ⃝ full stop B ⃝ exclamation mark

    C ⃝ question mark D ⃝ comma

Grammar Level 1 Quiz 5

It's a tricky one! Unjumble the words and rearrange them to make a proper sentence.

1. I s   r o y u   d a d
   w g r n k i o   n w o ?

2. e A r   y o u   n a c t h i g w
   N x t i f l e ?

3. e A r   t h e   i r g s l
   d g n n c i a ?

4. I s   t R e o b r
   g s i i n I n t e   o t
   s i c u m ?

5. I s   t h e   d o g
   r g n n n i u ?

6. e A r   S a m   a n d   T m o
   s i n g n g i ?

7. I s   o u r   c a t
   I n i s e e p g ?

8. e A r   y h t e
   n w m i m i g s   n i   t e h
   s e a ?

9. I s   L e a   n h t a t i g c
   o t   h r e   a t e e r c h ?

27

Grammar Level 1 Quiz 6

💡 Here's a few more SPAG questions.

1. Click on the correct word to complete the sentence. **We were_____ on our topics.**

   A ⬡ worked　　　　B ⬡ works

   C ⬡ working　　　　D ⬡ work

2. Click on the correct word to complete the sentence in the past tense. **I _____to Scotland during the school holidays.**

   A ⬡ go　　　　　　B ⬡ going

   C ⬡ went　　　　　D ⬡ was

3. Click on the correct word to complete the sentence. **Tomorrow, we could go for a walk _____play games indoors.**

   A ⬡ when　　　　　B ⬡ or

   C ⬡ because　　　　D ⬡ if

4. Click on the correct word to complete the sentence. **_____ you go to the park, you can play a game.**

   A ⬡ And　　　　　　B ⬡ So

   C ⬡ But　　　　　　D ⬡ If

5. Which sentence is a command?

   A ⬡ Pack away your paints now.

   B ⬡ You should be proud of your work.

   C ⬡ Will you show me your painting?

   D ⬡ That's your best work yet!

6. Choose the correct suffix to add to the word fall in this sentence. **The autumn leaves are fall___ to the ground.**

   A ⬡ ed　　　　　　B ⬡ s

   C ⬡ est　　　　　　D ⬡ ing

7. Choose a suffix to add to the word fast in this sentence. **The hare knew that he could run fast___ than the tortoise.**

   A ⬡ er　　　　　　B ⬡ est

   C ⬡ ing　　　　　　D ⬡ ed

8. What type of word is in **bold** in this sentence? "Gran thought the flowers were **pretty**."

   A ⬡ noun　　　　　B ⬡ verb

   C ⬡ adjective　　　D ⬡ adverb

9. In this sentence, why does Saturday, Sarah and Scotland have a capital letter? On **Saturday** morning, **Sarah** and her family went on holiday to **Scotland**.

   A ⬡ They are nouns　　B ⬡ they are proper nouns

   C ⬡ they are adjectives　D ⬡ at the beginning of a sentence.

10. How many nouns are in this sentence? **You have left your pencil on the bench over there.**

    A ⬡ 1　　　　　　B ⬡ 2

    C ⬡ 3　　　　　　D ⬡ 4

11. What type of sentence is this? **One day, Ali decided to make a toy robot.**

    A ⬡ a question　　　B ⬡ a statement

    C ⬡ a command　　　D ⬡ an exclamation

12. Which word is an adverb in this sentence? **Jamie knocked softly on his brother's bedroom door.**

    A ⬡ knocked　　　　B ⬡ door

    C ⬡ softly　　　　　D ⬡ brother

13. Which sentence uses an apostrophe correctly?

    A ⬡ Lucy's bag is green and has lots of pockets.

    B ⬡ Lucys' bag is green and has lots of pockets.

    C ⬡ Lucys bag is green and has lot's of pockets.

    D ⬡ Lucys bag is green and has lots of pocket's.

14. Which sentence uses a comma correctly?

    A ⬡ The museum shop sell,s posters mugs and badges.

    B ⬡ The museum, shop sells posters mugs an badges.

    C ⬡ The museum shop sells posters mugs, and badges.

    D ⬡ The museum shop sells posters, mugs and badges.

15. Which punctuation mark completes the sentence? **What a wonderful present you gave me**

    A ⬡ full stop　　　　B ⬡ exclamation mark

    C ⬡ question mark　　D ⬡ comma

SENTENCES

Writing a sentence should be straight forward, but many students struggle with some of the basics. A simple sentence always needs a **Subject** (the person or thing DOING the action) and a **Verb** (the action). Sentences may also have an **Object** (the receiver of the action - the one it is being done to).

So, every full sentence must have a DOER and an ACTION. **John** (the doer) **ate** (the action) **a cake** (the object or receiver of the action).

A sentence MUST start with a CAPITAL LETTER and end with a FULL STOP. (unless it ends with an Exclamation mark! or a question mark? There are no excuses for not starting with a capital letter and ending with a full stop. The examiner will deduct points.

Active sentences are a fundamental aspect of good writing. Writing in the active voice can make your sentences more engaging, direct, and powerful. In contrast, passive sentences can make your writing seem vague, unenthusiastic, and confusing. Active sentences are those in which the **subject** of the sentence **performs the action**, while passive sentences are those in which the subject receives the action. For example:

Active sentence: The dog chased the ball.
Passive sentence: The ball was chased by the dog.

In the active sentence, the subject (the dog) is performing the action (chased), while in the passive sentence, the subject (the ball) is receiving the action (was chased).

Active sentences are often more concise and clear than passive sentences. Try to use them.

Passive sentence: The cake was eaten by the children.
Active sentence: The children ate the cake.

In your writing tasks try to put two sentences together to make one long sentence. Examiners love it when you link two sentences together - using linking words (conjunctions) like: **AND, BUT or BECAUSE.**

The team wrote the report and delivered it to the coach.

My brother drove the car, but he didn't have a license.

The author wrote the book because it had always been his dream.

In the exam, try to write longer sentences and use longer words.

Sentence Level 1 Quiz 1

💡 Only one sentence is correct. See if you can find which is most grammatically correct.

1. She doesn't
   - A ☐ to the doctor go
   - B ☐ go to the doctor
   - C ☐ the doctor go

2. I like
   - A ☐ it because it's healthy
   - B ☐ because healthy
   - C ☐ because healthy is

3. Next week
   - A ☐ to Newport I'll go
   - B ☐ I'll to Newport go
   - C ☐ I'll go to Newport

4. I want
   - A ☐ job doctor
   - B ☐ future job doctor
   - C ☐ to be a doctor

5. My daughter
   - A ☐ wants to go to school
   - B ☐ wants school
   - C ☐ want go school

6. Jasmin says
   - A ☐ she went to the zoo tomorrow
   - B ☐ she went to the zoo yesterday
   - C ☐ she may go to the zoo last week
   - D ☐ she will definitely go to the zoo last Friday

7. Yanni needs to go and buy
   - A ☐ summet for tea
   - B ☐ some groceries yesterday
   - C ☐ some: milk, bread, and cheese

8. If you work hard in college
   - A ☐ there are lots of nice people there
   - B ☐ there is a great cafe
   - C ☐ you will learn a lot

9. He needs three shirts
   - A ☐ so he will bought some next week
   - B ☐ so he will brought them from a shop
   - C ☐ so he will need to save up some money

10. She gave a
    - A ☐ through account of her actions
    - B ☐ though account of her actions
    - C ☐ thorough account of her actions

30

Sentence Level 1 Quiz 2

💡 Write in the item numbers of the correct and incorrect sentences. Especially look how each sentence starts and how it ends.

Correct ☐☐☐☐ ☐☐☐

Incorrect ☐☐☐☐ ☐☐☐

1

The elephants needed help because they were hurt.

2

the selfish baboon kept all the coconuts.

3

After that, the happy giant smiled and gave Jack his golden egg.

4

Last night, the dog .

5

Soon, the.

6

After that, the happy giant smiled and gave egg

7

Suddenly, the elephants needed help.

8

Soon, the elephants were charging at me.

9

Last night, the dog barked loudly.

10

Last night, the dog barked loudly

11

Elephants needed help came

12

The were charging at me.

13

the elephants needed help because they were hurt

14

Suddenly, the elephants needed help but no-one came.

15

Next, the baboon kept all the coconuts because he was greedy.

31

What on earth are organisational features or organisational techniques? These are two terms the examiners like to use at both Level 1 and Level 2. They just mean LAYOUT. They are referring to the way the information is laid out on the page.

Some examples of organisational features are:

Paragraphs - Headings/Titles - Italics Sub Headings - Bullet Points - Images - Captions - Text Boxes - Chronological Order - Tables - Graphs - Charts - Bold Text - Numbered List - Speech Bubble

Think about ways the author of a the text has chosen to lay out their writing - so that it is easier to read and understand. Organisational features make it easier to read by adding visual elements to break up the writing.

You may be asked to **"Identify what organisational features the writer has used in this text."** Make sure you know the many ways text can be organised. Look at a typical newspaper and all the ways the publisher uses to tell a story. There will be a headline, maybe a sub heading, a large image with a caption, quotes may be separated into a box, and there may be charts showing statistics.

When using these organisational features you must think about your audience. 'Who is reading what I am writing?' Then, you can determine what elements will help your readers understand your message more clearly. If you are writing a scientific journal then using data charts and graphs may be helpful. If you are writing a children's book, then lots of images and illustrations are necessary.

Instead of a weather person just reading what the weather forecast is going to be over the next few days, they use a map of the UK, with symbols showing if it going to be sunny, or rainy, and they have numbers on the screen indicating high and low temperatures. They may even have arrows indicating wind direction. These visual elements are similar to what a writer would use to explain the text.

The examiner might also ask, **"Why has the author used these organisational features?"** Be prepared to look at text with a critical eye, and understand the reasoning behind using different layout features.

Organisational Features Level 1 Quiz 1

💡 Can you match up the organisational features?

1. Small symbols, often black circles, used to list items

A. speech bubble
B. paragraph
C. bullet points
D. webpage tab

2. A box with a border (separate from the main text)

A. title/heading
B. text box
C. bullet points
D. column

3. Additional information at the bottom of the page

A. text box
B. image
C. footnote
D. home icon

4. A box with rows and columns (containing information)

A. table
B. browser bar
C. column
D. bullet points

5. Words which are darker/heavier

A. column
B. hyperlink
C. bold font
D. browser bar

6. Inform the reader what the text is about

A. browser bar
B. bold font
C. title/heading
D. italics

Memorise the terms organisational features and organisational techniques so that you can recognise them on the exam.

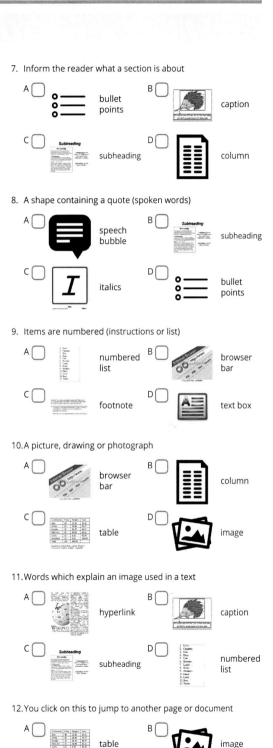

7. Inform the reader what a section is about

A. bullet points
B. caption
C. subheading
D. column

8. A shape containing a quote (spoken words)

A. speech bubble
B. subheading
C. italics
D. bullet points

9. Items are numbered (instructions or list)

A. numbered list
B. browser bar
C. footnote
D. text box

10. A picture, drawing or photograph

A. browser bar
B. column
C. table
D. image

11. Words which explain an image used in a text

A. hyperlink
B. caption
C. subheading
D. numbered list

12. You click on this to jump to another page or document

A. table
B. image
C. hyperlink
D. caption

13. Vertical blocks of text (side by side on a page)

A ☐ 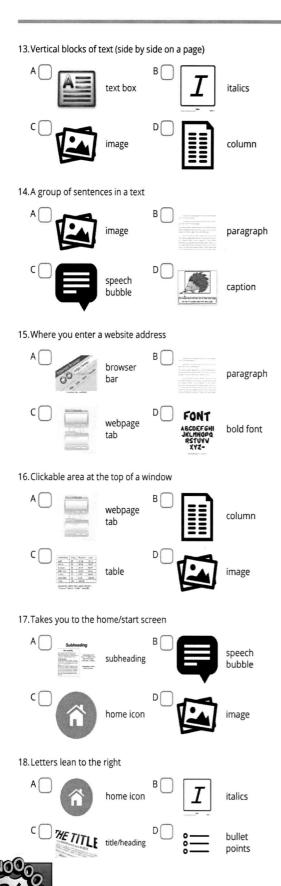 text box

B ☐ *I* italics

C ☐ image

D ☐ column

14. A group of sentences in a text

A ☐ image

B ☐ paragraph

C ☐ speech bubble

D ☐ caption

15. Where you enter a website address

A ☐ browser bar

B ☐ paragraph

C ☐ webpage tab

D ☐ **FONT** ABCDEFGHI JKLMNOPQ RSTUVW XYZ- bold font

16. Clickable area at the top of a window

A ☐ webpage tab

B ☐ column

C ☐ table

D ☐ image

17. Takes you to the home/start screen

A ☐ subheading

B ☐ speech bubble

C ☐ home icon

D ☐ image

18. Letters lean to the right

A ☐ home icon

B ☐ *I* italics

C ☐ *THE TITLE* title/heading

D ☐ bullet points

Look at this magazine cover. Ask yourself 'what elements stand out?' What catches your eye? Many of the organisational features we have discussed briefly are included here.

The image is iconic. This cover shows midwives from the BBC TV drama, 'Call the Midwife.' They are in front of a Christmas tree, holding babies. This is a striking image.

But, there are also headlines/titles, and bold text is used, in colour to stand out. There are words written in all capital letters, and there are also image boxes along the bottom of the cover.

At the top, there is another image of a British comedian wrapped in Christmas decorations. All these different organisational features help to sell the magazine to prospective buyers and are powerful tools the publisher uses to attract readers.

FORMAT

Choosing the right format when you write is essential. You probably send text messages to your friends, using 'text speak.' But, in the business world, and for your Functional Skills English exams, you may be asked to write a formal letter or an email. These will probably be very formal, perhaps a letter to the local council, or an email to a business assoicate. Whatever you are asked to write, you need to know the format, and know it well. For this book, we will just concentrate on the formal letter and the formal email, but you may also be asked to write a review, or a blog, a diary entry, or an eyewitness report. Look up the format of each so that you are prepared. Please note that although the format differs with each, the content is very similar in how it is set out.

When writing, we follow an IPPPC format. This means that, after getting the format at the top of your document correct, the body of your text will go as follows:

INTRODUCTION - This is where you get to the point of your communication. Why are you writing this letter or email? You do not need to say, "Hello, I'm Patrick...." Your name is already on the letter or email - so don't write that. Also, DON'T WRITE, "I am writing to you because.... Or, "I am sending you this email because." They have the letter or email in front of them, so you don't need to explain what it is...get right to the point.

"I would like to apply for the job as caretakeer at your college......"
"I would like to apply for a scholarship....."

PARAGRAPH 1 - This is where you outline the situation. Give facts here. Tell about the night you visited their restaurant, about the dinner served, about what happened that caused you to write.

PARAGRAPH 2 - This is where you elaborate and give more evidence, more information, where you build your case, or tell more about yourself and your qualifications.

PARAGRAPH 3 - This is where you might talk about how this situation made you and your group FEEL. Yes, you can bring emotion in here. What affect did the situation have upon you?

CONCLUSION or CALL TO ACTION - This is where you tell the person what you want to happen next. What do you want them to do, and by when? Do they need to respond to your request within so many days? Can they call you? If so, be sure to put your phone number at the bottom of the message.

It might sound like a lot of paragraphs to write, but the exam may ask you to write 200 or 250 words, so you do have to keep on writing. If you fail to write what the examiner asks of you - you will have points deducted.

Letter Level 1 Quiz 1

Draw a line from each of the elements of the letter to the position they should go.

Here is a letter and an email for you to format. Draw your lines in pencil, and have a go. It may take you a few times before you get all the format elements in the right order. Keep practicing. You will need to know this exact format. Please note that in an email you sign off, "Regards" or "Kind Regards" - do not use faithfully or sincerely.

Sender's address (your address)

Date

Name and address of recipient

Greeting (Dear Sir/Madam,)

Greeting (Dear Ms Chapman,)

Introduction (The main reason you are writing)

Main Paragraph 1

Main Paragraph 2

Main Paragraph 3

Closing paragraph (What you want to happen next)

Sign off (Yours Faithfully...)

Sign off (Yours Sincerely...)

Sender's name

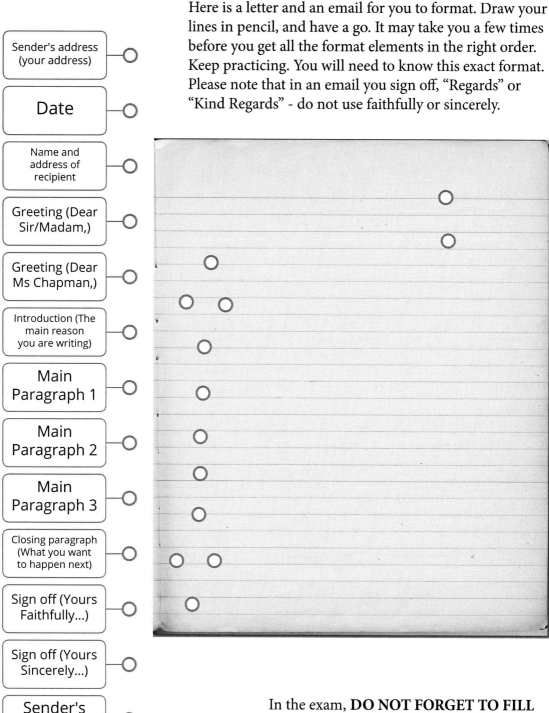

In the exam, **DO NOT FORGET TO FILL OUT THE SUBJECT LINE of the Email.** You will lose a point if you forget the subject.

Email Level 1 Quiz 1

Draw a line from each of the elements of an email to the correct position they should be on the email.

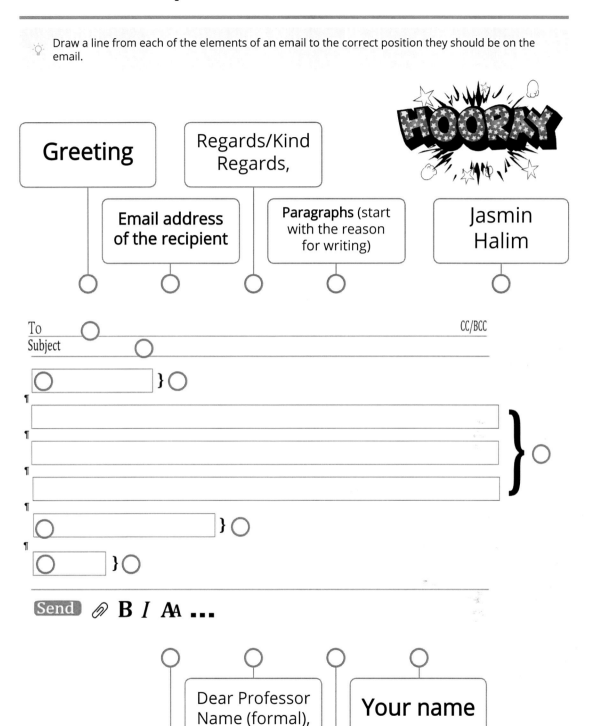

Greeting

Regards/Kind Regards,

Email address of the recipient

Paragraphs (start with the reason for writing)

Jasmin Halim

To   CC/BCC
Subject

Send   B *I* AA ...

Dear Professor Name (formal),

Your name

Clear and Concise Subject

Sign off

One of the ways writers create a scene in your mind is by using language features to describe or draw comparisons to other things in normal life that you can picture, or by playing with words and sounds. to conjure up feelings. Let's have a look at some of the most common, and easier-to-use examples that you might begin to employ in your writing. If you can use Language Features at Level 1 and Level 2, you will earn extra points.

Rhetorical Question: Asking a question that does not require a direct answer; it is asked just to make people think, to stimulate the conversation.

Example1: "What time do you call this?!"
Example 2: "Do you really want the people in Africa to starve?"

Using a rhetorical question at the start, or at the very end of a text can be a very powerful tool.

Simile: A comparison between two different things using "like" or "as"

Example 1: "Her hair was as black as coal." (The color of her hair is compared to coal using "as".)
Example 2: "He runs like a cheetah chasing its prey." (The way he runs is compared to a cheetah using "like".)

Metaphor: A comparison between two different things without using "like" or "as"

Example 1: "Life is a journey." (Life is compared to a journey, implying that both have ups and downs, twists and turns.)
Example 2: "The world is a stage." (The world is compared to a stage, implying that people play different roles in life.)

Personification: Giving human characteristics to non-human things

Example 1: "The wind whispered through the trees." (The wind is given the human characteristic of whispering.)
Example 2: "The sun smiled down on us." (The sun is given the human characteristic of smiling.)

Hyperbole: An exaggeration used to emphasize a point

Example 1: "I've told you a million times!" (The number of times the speaker has repeated themselves is exaggerated for emphasis.)
Example 2: "She was so hungry, she could have eaten a horse." (The level of hunger is exaggerated to emphasize how hungry she was.)

Alliteration: The repetition of the same sound at the beginning of words

Example 1: "Peter Piper picked a peck of pickled peppers." (The "p" sound is repeated throughout the sentence.)
Example 2: "She sells seashells by the seashore." (The "s" sound is repeated throughout the sentence.)

Onomatopoeia: Words that imitate the sound they describe

Example 1: "The clock tick-tocked in the silent room." (The word "tick-tocked" imitates the sound of a clock.)
Example 2: "The thunder roared in the distance." (The word "roared" imitates the sound of thunder.)

Irony: A contrast between what is expected and what actually happens

Example 1: "A fire station burns down." (The place that is meant to prevent fires actually catches fire.)
Example 2: "The traffic jam clears up just as you arrive at your destination." (The traffic jam causes the speaker to be delayed, but it clears up as soon as they arrive.)

Symbolism: The use of an object or image to represent an idea or concept

Example 1: The American flag represents freedom and democracy. (The flag represents larger concepts than just cloth and colors.)
Example 2: The dove is a symbol of peace. (The bird represents a larger concept of peace.)

Repetition: The repeating of a word or phrase for emphasis

Example 1: "I have a dream that one day this nation will rise up and live out the true meaning of its creed." (The phrase "I have a dream" is repeated for emphasis.)

Example 2: "We shall fight on the beaches, we shall fight on the landing grounds, we shall fight in the fields and in the streets."(The phrase "we shall fight" is repeated for emphasis.)

Rule of Three: Where three words or phrases within the same group can be used together

Example 1: Hands, Face, Space
Example 2: Stop, Look and Listen

Here's a quick quiz to see if you remember some of the literary features/techniques we have covered. These are just a few. When you have mastered them, look up more examples of literary techniques or language features, such as using humour. We've made this quiz easy - by giving you the answers underneath each question, but try to see how well you do - without looking.

What is a simile?
a) A comparison between two different things without using "like" or "as"
b) A comparison between two different things using "like" or "as"
c) Giving human characteristics to non-human things

Answer: b) A comparison between two different things using "like" or "as"

What is a metaphor?
a) A comparison between two different things without using "like" or "as"
b) A comparison between two different things using "like" or "as"
c) Giving human characteristics to non-human things

Answer: a) A comparison between two different things without using "like" or "as"

What is personification?
a) A comparison between two different things without using "like" or "as"
b) A comparison between two different things using "like" or "as"
c) Giving human characteristics to non-human things

Answer: c) Giving human characteristics to non-human things

What is hyperbole?
a) The repetition of the same sound at the beginning of words
b) The repetition of vowel sounds within words
c) An exaggeration used to emphasize a point

Answer: c) An exaggeration used to emphasize a point

What is alliteration?
a) The repetition of the same sound at the beginning of words
b) The repetition of vowel sounds within words
c) Words that imitate the sound they describe

Answer: a) The repetition of the same sound (not always the same letter) at the beginning of words

What is onomatopoeia?
a) The repetition of the same sound at the beginning of words
b) The repetition of vowel sounds within words
c) Words that imitate the sound they describe

Answer: c) Words that imitate the sound they describe

What is irony?
a) Giving human characteristics to non-human things
b) An exaggeration used to emphasize a point
c) A contrast between what is expected and what actually happens

Answer: c) A contrast between what is expected and what actually happens

What is symbolism?
a) A comparison between two different things without using "like" or "as"
b) Descriptive language that appeals to the senses
c) The use of an object or image to represent an idea or concept

Answer: c) The use of an object or image to represent an idea or concept

What is repetition?
a) Giving a hint or suggestion of what is to come later in the story
b) The repeating of a word or phrase for emphasis
c) A scene that interrupts the narrative to show an event that happened earlier in time

Answer: b) The repeating of a word or phrase for emphasis

What is the Rule of Three?
a) Three separate people mentioned within a paragraph
b) Using three related words to make your point
c) Using three metaphors in one paragraph

Answer: b) Using three related words to make your point

What is tone?
a) The attitude or mood conveyed by the author's writing
b) A comparison between two different things without using "like" or "as"
c) Giving human characteristics to non-human things

Answer: a) The attitude or mood conveyed by the author's writing

What literary technique is used in the sentence "The wind whispered through the trees"?
a) Simile
b) Metaphor
c) Personification

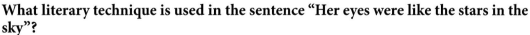

Answer: c) Personification

What literary technique is used in the sentence "Her eyes were like the stars in the sky"?
a) Simile
b) Metaphor
c) Personification

Answer: a) Simile

What literary technique is used in the sentence "My father was a rock in my life"?
a) Simile
b) Metaphor
c) Personification

Answer: c) Metaphor

What literary technique is used in the sentence "The sun smiled down on us"?
a) Simile
b) Metaphor
c) Personification

Answer: c) Personification

What literary technique is used in the sentence "The thunder roared like a lion"?
a) Simile
b) Metaphor
c) Personification

Answer: a) Simile

As you can imagine, using these language tricks to create a picture, describe a feeling or a character, or even create an emotional response in your reader, can be powerful.

Mastering Language Techniques or Langauge Features will bring your writing to life. This is used all the time in long-form writing, where a reader invites you to share a deeper engagement, giving you time to set a scene, and to introduce and develop characters.

In the English exam you may be asked to *"identify what language features have been used in the text."* It may ask you to identify up to three separate language features, so it's important to memorise some of them.

Some of the most often used Language Features in the exams are:

Direct Address: "**You** do this, **you** should do that."

First Person: "**I** did this, **I** did that."

Simile: "She walked **like** a duck."

Metaphor: "He **was** her **rock**." "He **is** my **rock**."

Personification "The **wind whistled** round the tree."

Language Features Level 1 Quiz 1

💡 Find the Language Features. They can be Up, Down, Across or Diagonal

1. Rhetorical Question
2. Alliteration
3. Rule of three
4. Simile
5. Metaphor
6. Humour
7. Direct Address
8. First Person

R	F	N	U	A	W	V	O	W	W	L	N	V	D	L	T	N	J	R
R	D	E	H	L	U	V	K	T	I	O	J	Q	A	Z	O	S	J	X
M	H	L	B	I	O	Q	E	M	I	X	Y	P	L	S	E	I	L	N
E	U	K	L	W	G	K	V	T	S	D	V	J	R	E	N	M	E	D
T	M	B	H	N	P	V	A	F	Y	X	K	E	R	N	M	I	U	C
A	O	U	F	E	Z	R	B	B	W	D	P	H	B	U	D	L	G	V
P	U	R	Q	Y	E	P	B	Z	J	T	T	K	V	I	E	E	E	T
H	R	Y	L	T	V	U	Q	J	S	F	N	C	P	D	E	H	R	R
O	S	P	I	A	G	E	N	R	O	Z	R	D	J	D	J	I	D	W
R	K	L	S	V	Z	V	I	E	L	X	U	I	M	E	V	Y	U	W
X	L	F	Y	N	T	F	L	J	L	W	G	W	Y	P	B	B	Y	O
A	J	Y	P	O	S	U	Q	B	N	R	V	P	F	H	B	J	P	K
M	C	G	R	A	R	E	O	C	B	B	J	D	B	G	O	W	M	X
Y	R	H	E	T	O	R	I	C	A	L	Q	U	E	S	T	I	O	N
D	T	T	Q	C	T	G	T	R	S	A	F	I	V	C	C	L	V	K
C	R	R	Z	P	W	Z	X	U	Z	Y	E	F	R	H	C	Q	D	E
X	Q	O	R	T	Y	D	I	R	E	C	T	A	D	D	R	E	S	S
T	E	E	O	Z	U	L	D	L	T	A	D	V	T	V	D	J	A	D
Z	I	N	M	M	R	Y	E	N	B	R	Y	U	F	O	C	A	R	Y

Language Features Level 1 Quiz 2

💡 Rearrange these letters to spell out the correct Language Features.

1. i D t c e r
   s s a e d r d
   ☐☐☐☐☐☐
   ☐☐☐☐☐☐

2. S e s l i i m
   ☐☐☐☐☐☐☐

3. o e i p R n e t t i
   ☐☐☐☐☐☐☐☐☐☐

4. p e h M o t r a
   ☐☐☐☐☐☐☐☐

5. o n s P o r f n i c e i a t i
   ☐☐☐☐☐☐☐☐☐☐☐☐☐☐☐

6. u e R l   f o   e r t h e
   ☐☐☐☐ ☐☐
   ☐☐☐☐☐

7. a h r e R l t i o c
   s e i o t n u q
   ☐☐☐☐☐☐☐☐☐☐
   ☐☐☐☐☐☐☐

8. i s s L t
   ☐☐☐☐☐

9. e n i l o a t A t r i l
   ☐☐☐☐☐☐☐☐☐☐☐☐

10. i p o O n i s n
    ☐☐☐☐☐☐☐☐

11. e b e H p l o y r
    ☐☐☐☐☐☐☐☐☐

12. a s c F t
    ☐☐☐☐☐

13. c t s a S s t t i i
    ☐☐☐☐☐☐☐☐☐☐

14. E v e i t m o
    g n a g u e a l
    ☐☐☐☐☐☐☐☐
    ☐☐☐☐☐☐☐

15. t a e o i p o O a o m n
    ☐☐☐☐☐☐☐☐☐☐☐☐

Language Features Level 1 Quiz 3

💡 Draw a line to match the definition with the Language Feature

Direct address	3 describing words in a list
Triple/list of 3/ rule of 3	A question that doesn't need an answer
Simile	Sound effect words
Onomatopoeia	Describes how something is
Rhetorical question	A doing word
Adjective	Comparison using LIKE or AS
Hyperbole	Saying something IS something that it can't literally be
Alliteration	Talking at the reader using 'you'
Metaphor	3 (or more) words in a sentence with the same starting letter
Personification	Giving a non-human human qualities
Adverb	Over-exaggeration for effect
Verb	Describes how something is done

FORMAL V INFORMAL

You probably speak informally, most of us do. You use simple sentences made up of simple words, and you get to the point as quickly as possible. You very rarely come across someone who talks to you in a very formal way, using elongated words and complex sentences that are sometimes difficult to understand. Life would be hard for us all if we had to concentrate on every single word to try to find meaning in someone's speech. Life is too short.

But, on the other hand, in a world of 'text speak' abbreviated words can often leave the uninitiated confused. The younger age groups - including probably yourself, have 'text speak' down to an art, and it behooves older folk to get on board or they will be left in the dark - not having a clue what their younger counterparts are saying. So, there are several forms of informal language - the way most of us speak, slang, text speak and language based on culture. The words and abbreviations often used in texts are similar to ones used in conversation by older generations - but may have vastly different meanings.

These abbreviations, to fit the limited number of characters allowed on some messaging services, are probably very familiar. But be aware that many people do not have a clue what they mean:

10Q - Thank you
2M2H - Too much to handle
AAS - Alive and smiling
AQAP - As quickly as possible
DBBSWF - Dream boat body, Shipwreck face
MUAH - Multiple unsuccessful attempts at humour
PLOS -Parents looking over the shoulder

In some forms of communication, formal writing is essential. For most business situations, letters and legal documents are often written very formally. Think of contracts, to rent an apartment, or even to sign up with a mobile carrier, or a movie streaming service; they are mostly written formally. This is because they are legal documents, and anytime it's legal, there's a whole lot of verbiage that needs to be included, much of which we 'regular people' don't understand.

You will be required on many occasions - surprisingly many occasions - to write formally. You might have to write to a college enquiring about a course of study, a council to complain, apply for a job, to include a cover letter when returning a product. Yes, in a world where we think 'no one writes letters anymore' - there are quite a few times when you will have to put pen to paper, or at least type on a keyboard - a formal piece of written communication. So, you must be able to differentiate between formal and informal writing. Let us commence.(Formal) Here we go! (Informal)

SLANG/Very Informal	INFORMAL/normal	FORMAL
Piddly		
Chuffed		
Bevy		
Specs		
Bloke		
Ace		
Mate		
Pick your brains		
Shut up		
Kid		
Digs		

Formal Text Rules:
- Uses standard grammar rules and vocabulary.
- Avoids contractions (say 'do not', not don't, say 'could not', not couldn't) and slang.
- Uses full sentences and avoids fragments.
- Avoids personal pronouns (e.g. "I", "we", "you") and instead uses third-person pronouns (e.g. "he", "she", "they").
- Follows a specific format or structure, such as in academic papers, legal documents, or business letters.
- Uses more technical or specialized vocabulary.
- Usually written to people we do not know.

Informal Text Rules:
- Uses slang and contractions.
- Uses shorter sentences and sentence fragments.
- Uses personal pronouns (e.g. "I", "we", "you") more freely.
- Includes idiomatic expressions and colloquialisms (local words).
- Can be more conversational in tone.
- Often used in text messages, social media posts, or personal emails.

Formal v Informal Level 1 Quiz 4

Only put a check under the INFORMAL moles

ACQUAINTANCE • VEHICLES • GENTLEMEN • ACE

ENQUIRE • PIDDLY • MATE • INSIGNIFICANT

DELIGHTED • WELL HAPPY • GRANNY • CHUFFED

RATHER SPLENDID • BLOKE • KID • SPECTACLES

SPECS • BEVERAGE • FUN

Formal v Informal Level 1 Quiz 2

💡 Write in the item numbers in the list of boxes for each group

Formal ◻◻◻◻◻◻◻◻◻◻◻◻

Informal ◻◻◻◻◻◻◻◻◻◻◻

1	2	3	4
See you soon.	With reference to your letter dated ...	I want to know about ...	Thanks for your letter.

5	6	7	8
I am writing to express my concerns.	Yours sincerely,	Yours faithfully,	Best wishes,

9	10	11	12
Lots of love.	Hi!	Dear Nanny and Grandad,	I got your letter.

13	14	15	16
Let me know if it's OK.	Please find enclosed ...	Give my love to ...	I'm writing to tell you that ...

17	18	19	20
To whom it may concern.	I look forward to hearing from you.	Dear Sir or Madam,	I would like to confirm that ...

21	22	23
I am writing to apply for the position of ...	Please contact me if you require any further information.	Dear Mrs Smith,

Formal v Informal Level 1 Quiz 3

💡 Choose the most appropriate answer for formal writing

1. In a formal letter, you will always write to someone you know

   A ☐ True   B ☐ False

2. What tone should a formal letter always have?

   A ☐ forceful   B ☐ appropriate and polite   C ☐ patronising

3. If you do not know the recepient's name, your formal letter should always end

   A ☐ Yours sincerely   B ☐ Yours with love   C ☐ Yours faithfully

4. Your formal letter should always include

   A ☐ a long opening paragraph

   B ☐ a brief opening paragraph which introduces your reason for writing

   C ☐ bullet points with the main reasons for writing

5. The person you are writing to

   A ☐ purpose   B ☐ content

   C ☐ audience   D ☐ format

6. The reason you are writing a formal letter

   A ☐ purpose   B ☐ content

   C ☐ audience   D ☐ format

7. The layout of a formal letter

   A ☐ purpose   B ☐ content

   C ☐ audience   D ☐ format

8. The topic of your letter

   A ☐ purpose   B ☐ content

   C ☐ audience   D ☐ format

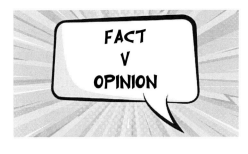

**FACT
V
OPINION**

We live in a world now where facts and opinions seem interchangeable, where it's often difficult to determine fact from fiction, and where previously reliable sources now flaunt infotainment as news, and officials openly present "alternative facts." But, let's be clear that facts and opinions are two distinctly different beasts, and should be handled with care.

- A fact is a statement that can be proven true or false based on objective evidence or data. Facts are verifiable and do not change based on personal beliefs or feelings. For example, "The Earth revolves around the Sun" is a fact that can be proven through scientific evidence.

- An opinion is a personal belief or judgment about a topic or issue. Opinions are subjective and can vary from person to person. They are often based on personal experiences, values, or beliefs, and are not necessarily based on objective evidence or data. For example, "Chocolate ice cream is the best flavour" is an opinion, as it is based on personal preference rather than objective evidence.

Generally, you can spot true information if it contains:

**STATISTICS
NUMBERS
DATES
EVENTS
HISTORICAL
NON-FICTION**

and is said by an authority, such as:

**A PROFESSIONAL OR EXPERT IN THAT FIELD
A PROFESSIONAL BODY/ORGANISATION
A SCHOOL, UNIVERSITY, OR OTHER EDUCATIONAL FACILITY
RESEARCH BODY
AN OFFICIAL REPORT**

But, be aware that even professionals, speaking about an area they know a lot about - STILL HAVE AN OPINION. Be careful to differentiate between the factual information they may have to share, from their own opinion on the matter. Remember, almost everyone has some kind of agenda, some form of bias, whether openly or hidden and that they may not even be aware they are pushing that agenda or opinion. The exam may ask you to *"find and describe the difference between fact and opinion in the text."*

You really need to be a full-on detective, looking for clues to pick out the fact from the fiction, or fact from opinion. The golden rule to ask yourself when reading, or writing a text is:

Can this information be proven?

There are other clues you can look for. The use of ADJECTIVES is an absolute giveaway clue. Fact is not usually associated with lots of adjectives like:

Wonderful, Great, Best, Biggest, Smallest, Nicest... in fact, any word that ends in ...est is a clue that this piece of writing is an opinion. In addition to EST endings, also look for ER - such as Bigger, Better, Greater, etc.

"The new Jaguar XJS model is the fastEST car on the road!" It may well be a fast car, but unless this statement is followed up by some statistics that compare it to every other fast car currently available and considered a road car, then the statement is opinion.

Opinions can be easily recognised when they use words like:
THINK, BELIEVE, SUGGEST, PERHAPS, PROBABLY, USUALLY, TYPICALLY, SHOULD, and MUST. Opinions also use judgement words such as: GOOD, BAD, BEST, WORST, MOST, LEAST, TERRIBLE, FANTASTIC and AWFUL.

FUN

ALL JUST OPINIONS

**Bigger - Better - Stronger
Best - Greatest - Widest - Longest
Kindest - Nicest - Gentlest**

**"I believe that..."
"I think that..."**

**"It will change your life...."
"There's never been another one like it..."**

**Marvelous - Wonderful - Fantastic
Amazing - Brilliant - Awesome**

Fact v Opinion Level 1 Quiz 1

💡 Write in the item numbers in the list of boxes for each group

Fact ☐☐☐☐☐ ☐☐☐☐☐

Opinion ☐☐☐☐☐ ☐☐☐☐☐

1	2	3
The UK Prime Minister lives in Downing Street	10 Downing Street is better than the Whitehouse	English is boring

4	5	6
The BBC is funded by a licence fee	London is the capital of England	King Charles' mother was the Queen

7	8	9
Workers in the UK pay too much income tax	Manchester should be the capital of England	Facebook is better than X

10	11	12
Paris is the capital of France	The British are the most polite of all people	Donald Trump was the President

13	14	15
The BBC is biased	Apples and Oranges are fruit	Donald Trump was the best President

16	17	18
Workers in the UK pay income tax	There are 7 days in a week	Twitter is now called X

19	20
Apples are better than Oranges	King Charles is a better leader than the Queen

53

Fact v Opinion Level 1 Quiz 2

Match the statements to whether they are FACT or OPINION

Opinion	That baby shark song is so annoying .
Fact	Mushrooms taste bad.
Fact	Cats are better than dogs.
Opinion	It rains all the time in England
Fact	Westminster Abbey is in London
Opinion	Manchester United is the best football team.
Opinion	Pizza is better than Pasta
Opinion	Hanoi is the capital of Vietnam.
Opinion	Buckingham Castle is just a big church in London
Opinion	Pasta is much tastier than pizza.
Fact	Spiders have more legs than me.
Opinion	June is a month.

54

Fact v Opinion Level 1 Quiz 3

Put a check below each of the moles that have a FACT.

Boston is famous for the pilgrims	Leeds has a University	Cabbage is Horrible	Climate change is real
Miami has the best beach	Too many people live in Manchester	The Earth is roundish	TV's future is bleak
Florida has sandy beaches	Some people like jazz music	Teens are watching less traditional television	The Earth is overpopulated
Broadcast TV is losing viewers	Cabbage can be Green	Teens should watch less television	Everyone should love brass bands
Leeds University is brilliant	Boston is officially boring	Save the planet today, or we're all going to die	Manchester is a City

Fact v Opinion Level 1 Quiz 4

💡 Match the statements to the matching FACT or OPINION image

1. Marge Simpson's maiden name is Bouvier

   A ⬜ Fact   B ⬜ Opinion
   C ⬜ Fact   D ⬜ Fact

2. Studies have shown that playing slow background music can make you eat food at a slower rate.

   A ⬜ Fact   B ⬜ Fact
   C ⬜ Fact   D ⬜ Fact

3. Manchester United are a much better football team than Chelsea.

   A ⬜ Opinion   B ⬜ Opinion
   C ⬜ Opinion   D ⬜ Opinion

4. Elton John's single, Candle in the Wind (Princess Diana tribute version) sold over 37 million copies worldwide, making it one of the best-selling songs of all time.

   A ⬜ Opinion   B ⬜ Fact
   C ⬜ Fact   D ⬜ Fact

5. Dogs make better pets than cats.

   A ⬜ Fact   B ⬜ Opinion
   C ⬜ Opinion   D ⬜ Fact

6. It is ethically unacceptable to inflict suffering on one species in the hope of trying to help another.

   A ⬜ Fact   B ⬜ Opinion
   C ⬜ Fact   D ⬜ Opinion

7. Since its introduction in February 1935, more than 200 million Monopoly board games have been sold worldwide.

   A ⬜ Fact   B ⬜ Fact
   C ⬜ Opinion   D ⬜ Opinion

8. The intimidation and violent actions of anti-vivisection protesters are deplorable.

   A ⬜ Opinion   B ⬜ Fact
   C ⬜ Opinion   D ⬜ Opinion

And, here's a surprise you may find difficult to accept about OPINION. Even if someone you really trust gives you a new piece of information - it doesn't make it true! Your loved ones are not the authority on truth. They only share what they believe to be true, but if it cannot be proven - then it is only their opinion. Truth is always verifiable; can be proven.

SPELLING
LEVEL 1

Here's some words you are expected to know the spelling and meaning of in Level 1. There will be no actual spelling test during the exam, but you will be expected to define some words and you MUST be able to use a dictionary. Practice looking up some of these words in a dictionary.

principal principle apparent occupy applied draft draught prophet profit feet feat familiar heard herd amateur twelfth yacht particular attaches attached tomatoes restaurant conscious embarrass suggest boxes conscience either neither protein seize immediate deceive precede proceed caffeine leaves teamwork conceive ceiling perceive ought nought fought thought borough bridle bridal cemetery rhyme cities existence devise device disastrous foreign relevant knives lightning individual necessary muscle stomach buses interrupt brushes bored board mourning morning according awkward assent ascent descent dissent cereal serial symbol complement compliment complete lose loose bruise queen quest quiz liquid quill queue quit quick stationery stationary ancient neighbour babies everyday wary weary calves nuisance arches churches parties temperature sincere variety heroes interfere copies living alter altar leisure vegetable shoulder harass language programme profession provide persuade reception applies appearance adapted affect effect official specific verified secretary attempt equipped affected electrical security progress industry businesses awareness experiences achieve vehicle hygiene wellbeing duties freelance receive temporary complete bought brought recognise signature system office ethics employment practise practice self-employed career benefit example equipment identify consider evidence employer guidelines marketing advise advice function product plumber company customers lawyer physical cultural interview studio reproduce situation cration labour location occasions maintained explain survey nominate department communities produce structure exchange challenge research teacher retiring ability soldier personal workload developing salary evaluate strategy hazards background attaching

Spelling Level 1 Quiz 1

The next few pages contain spellings of words you are expected to know at Level 1

💡 Find the 20 words. They can be found up, down, across or diagonal.

1. principal	2. principle	3. apparent	4. occupy	5. draft
6. draught	7. prophet	8. profit	9. feet	10. feat
11. familiar	12. heard	13. herd	14. amateur	15. twelfth
16. yacht	17. particular	18. conscious	19. embarrass	20. suggest

```
S  A  S  C  W  P  F  E  E  T  K  Y  A  C  H  T
P  A  R  T  I  C  U  L  A  R  J  O  A  O  R  C
P  E  F  E  D  R  A  U  G  H  T  Y  D  Y  A  E
R  P  R  I  N  C  I  P  A  L  J  R  L  N  T  H
I  F  G  A  Z  F  B  E  K  A  E  J  E  I  T  H
N  Q  E  D  Q  A  C  M  D  H  W  S  F  F  P  I
C  U  O  A  H  P  O  B  G  S  I  O  L  B  J  C
I  H  W  B  T  A  N  A  S  S  R  E  I  H  F  D
P  S  H  A  N  P  S  R  U  P  W  D  X  E  L  R
L  H  L  M  P  P  C  R  G  T  R  G  J  A  D  A
E  P  K  A  R  A  I  A  G  N  H  M  Q  R  H  F
Y  H  M  T  O  R  O  S  E  M  D  B  L  D  S  T
M  K  A  E  P  E  U  S  S  S  R  D  C  Q  O  P
K  E  H  U  H  N  S  P  T  O  C  C  U  P  Y  N
P  Z  D  R  E  T  H  P  N  W  K  B  N  G  R  L
B  N  O  T  T  F  A  M  I  L  I  A  R  A  J  B
```

58

Spelling Level 1 Quiz 2

Rearrange these letters to spell out the correct words.

1. p i i n a r c p l

2. p i i n l r c p e

3. e a r p p a n t

4. c p u y o c

5. a r f t d

6. a d r t h u g

7. o p r t e p h

8. o i f t p r

9. f e e t

10. f a e t

11. i i l a m f a r

12. a e r d h

13. h r e d

14. a a m r u t e

15. e t w h t l f

16. c a h t y

17. a l t r i a p c r u

18. o n i s u o c c s

19. a b r a s m r e s

20. g s u t s g e

Spelling Level 1 Quiz 3

💡 Find the 20 words. They can be found up, down, across or diagonal.

1. either
2. neither
3. protein
4. seize
5. precede
6. proceed
7. caffeine
8. applied
9. attaches
10. attached
11. tomatoes
12. restaurant
13. conscience
14. immediate
15. teamwork
16. leaves
17. deceive
18. conceive
19. ceiling
20. perceive

R	K	A	V	X	G	V	C	J	M	Y	B	A	A	P	B	Y
E	C	D	M	C	P	S	A	E	H	T	W	V	T	R	A	R
S	E	R	N	O	E	F	F	Y	U	O	S	V	T	O	F	C
T	I	C	L	N	R	F	F	Y	S	M	V	A	A	T	B	U
A	L	I	M	C	C	X	E	L	X	A	W	D	C	E	C	X
U	I	E	J	E	E	R	I	E	V	T	E	N	H	I	O	T
R	N	A	A	I	I	S	N	A	I	O	D	J	E	N	N	A
A	G	T	X	V	V	P	E	V	W	E	F	N	S	L	S	N
N	I	E	S	E	E	R	F	E	P	S	P	O	J	E	C	V
T	M	A	E	P	A	O	K	S	U	V	G	T	W	T	I	U
Y	M	M	I	R	P	C	C	S	L	A	Y	V	E	Q	E	B
M	E	W	Z	E	P	E	B	N	E	I	T	H	E	R	N	D
W	D	O	E	C	L	E	D	E	C	E	I	V	E	I	C	W
Q	I	R	A	E	I	D	L	A	Q	L	Y	S	W	V	E	L
G	A	K	O	D	E	Y	P	A	T	T	A	C	H	E	D	E
K	T	D	X	E	D	J	Z	O	W	O	W	I	M	G	Q	K
D	E	E	I	T	H	E	R	H	D	S	S	S	K	C	W	B

Spelling Level 1 Quiz 4

☼ Rearrange these letters to spell out the correct words.

1. e i t r h e

2. t r e e h n i

3. t n i r e p o

4. e z e i s

5. c e d r e p e

6. c d e r e p o

7. f f i e e a n c

8. l d e p i a p

9. t a h s c t e a

10. t a h d c t e a

11. m a o s t o e t

12. t s r e r t a a n u

13. e n c o e s n c c i

14. i e m d t a e i m

15. a m o k w e r t

16. l e a s v e

17. e e v e i d c

18. n c i e e o v c

19. l g n e i c i

20. r c i e e e v p

Spelling Level 1 Quiz 5

Find the 20 words. They can be found up, down, across or diagonal.

1. ought	2. nought	3. fought	4. thought	5. borough
6. bridle	7. bridal	8. cemetery	9. rhyme	10. disastrous
11. foreign	12. relevant	13. individual	14. necessary	15. muscle
16. stomach	17. cities	18. knives	19. buses	20. brushes

```
C  T  H  O  U  G  H  T  L  E  C  K  D  K  F  A
M  U  S  C  L  E  N  C  P  G  M  P  I  P  M  C
N  E  C  E  S  S  A  R  Y  P  Y  D  S  C  O  E
W  M  P  F  O  U  G  H  T  K  B  Q  A  S  C  M
I  C  R  B  R  I  D  A  L  F  R  A  S  L  F  E
X  I  H  R  U  V  F  Q  X  Z  U  B  T  L  O  T
Z  N  Y  D  H  M  E  W  Q  I  S  O  R  J  R  E
W  D  M  K  N  I  V  E  S  Z  H  L  O  B  E  R
J  I  E  B  R  I  D  L  E  T  E  K  U  O  I  Y
T  V  U  G  W  L  C  M  L  K  S  H  S  R  G  A
A  I  C  G  C  I  T  I  E  S  G  E  G  O  N  Y
B  D  U  X  R  E  L  E  V  A  N  T  N  U  Z  H
U  U  H  O  U  G  H  T  A  B  E  Y  H  G  H  T
S  A  N  F  D  P  T  J  D  E  H  F  K  H  H  C
E  L  X  Y  Z  W  Y  F  H  N  O  U  G  H  T  P
S  L  S  K  M  H  H  X  E  S  T  O  M  A  C  H
```

Spelling Level 1 Quiz 6

Rearrange these letters to spell out the correct words.

1. t h o u g

2. n g t o h u

3. f g t o h u

4. h t h u g t o

5. g b o o u h r

6. b d e r l i

7. b d l r a i

8. e e c r m e t y

9. e m r h y

10. s r d u o s t s a i

11. g f o e i n r

12. e a r n l e v t

13. l d i a u d i v i n

14. s n y e s r e c a

15. m c e u l s

16. c s t m a h o

17. c i s i e t

18. k v s n e i

19. s e b u s

20. e b r s h s u

Spelling Level 1 Quiz 7

Find the 20 words. They can be found up, down, across or diagonal.

1. existence
2. lightning
3. interrupt
4. devise
5. device
6. awkward
7. assent
8. bored
9. board
10. mourning
11. morning
12. according
13. ascent
14. cereal
15. serial
16. symbol
17. complement
18. compliment
19. complete
20. bruise

I	G	W	O	I	T	W	L	M	X	C	X	Q	E	C	A	X
K	N	F	L	F	H	L	K	J	X	L	I	E	I	Q	C	I
H	R	T	C	O	M	P	L	E	T	E	D	W	T	H	C	B
B	C	A	E	Z	H	I	R	N	C	U	H	M	B	V	O	V
R	O	Q	W	R	S	L	I	G	H	T	N	I	N	G	R	A
U	M	E	Y	K	R	S	Y	M	B	O	L	E	Q	R	D	B
I	P	D	X	O	W	U	M	O	R	N	I	N	G	R	I	O
S	L	M	E	I	O	A	P	Z	F	R	O	H	G	R	N	A
E	I	A	A	V	S	B	R	T	X	N	Z	N	N	D	G	R
B	M	S	V	L	I	T	L	D	N	Q	I	F	H	E	I	D
W	E	S	E	K	S	S	E	H	N	N	H	E	Y	L	C	R
E	N	E	R	W	E	A	E	N	R	I	C	V	A	Q	X	D
F	T	N	R	A	D	R	S	U	C	I	W	I	K	W	E	W
G	W	T	Q	Q	X	V	O	C	V	E	R	N	G	R	N	V
Y	N	Y	S	A	T	M	X	E	E	E	D	Z	O	I	H	K
C	E	R	E	A	L	Z	D	C	S	N	F	B	B	V	A	G
E	C	O	M	P	L	E	M	E	N	T	T	X	O	L	Y	S

64

Spelling Level 1 Quiz 8

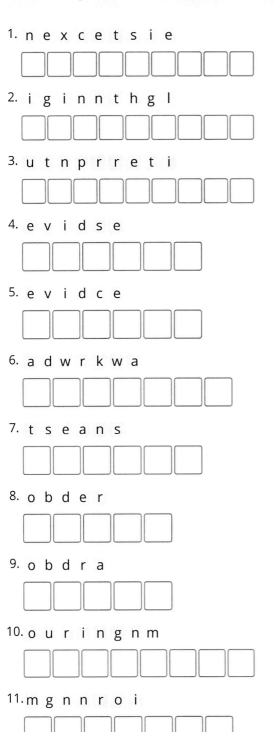

💡 Rearrange these letters to spell out the correct words.

1. n e x c e t s i e

2. i g i n n t h g l

3. u t n p r r e t i

4. e v i d s e

5. e v i d c e

6. a d w r k w a

7. t s e a n s

8. o b d e r

9. o b d r a

10. o u r i n g n m

11. m g n n r o i

12. i g c n d r o c a

13. t c e a n s

14. l r e c a e

15. l r i s a e

16. l m b s o y

17. t o l e p n m e m c

18. t o l e p n m i m c

19. o m p e t e l c

20. e u i b s r

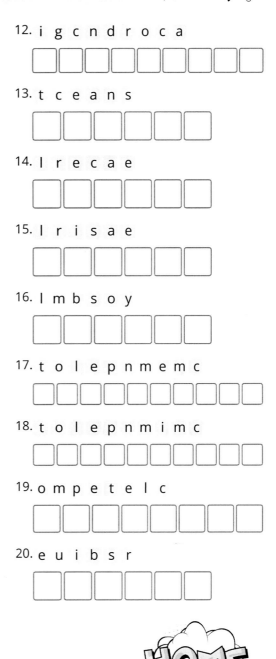

Spelling Level 1 Quiz 9

Find the 20 words. They can be found up, down, across or diagonal.

1. loose
2. lose
3. stationary
4. stationery
5. ancient
6. neighbour
7. everyday
8. wary
9. weary
10. nuisance
11. calves
12. temperature
13. parties
14. liquid
15. quest
16. queue
17. quick
18. quill
19. sincere
20. variety

D	J	F	N	U	I	S	A	N	C	E	E	T	Y	W	K
U	N	W	J	S	V	P	L	L	U	Q	Q	U	I	C	K
B	B	T	S	P	E	V	E	R	Y	D	A	Y	Y	V	I
T	I	E	E	H	L	L	K	T	S	S	P	R	Z	G	D
E	W	E	A	R	Y	W	N	E	E	Q	A	Z	V	Q	D
M	F	G	I	S	S	E	U	R	U	N	P	G	M	I	A
P	W	S	G	Q	I	T	K	X	O	L	U	T	U	S	C
E	L	V	J	C	Y	X	A	I	Q	G	C	Q	C	E	H
R	A	H	N	G	N	M	T	T	C	I	Y	S	W	E
A	A	A	V	R	R	A	P	S	I	L	A	O	G	R	O
T	Q	G	A	L	T	L	E	A	O	O	L	L	E	S	L
U	U	G	R	S	X	U	O	O	R	O	N	C	V	L	I
R	E	I	I	D	Q	A	V	O	P	T	N	E	I	E	F
E	U	N	E	I	Q	T	F	Y	S	I	I	U	R	W	S
H	E	Q	T	W	A	R	Y	J	S	E	Q	E	O	Y	N
L	Q	C	Y	N	E	I	G	H	B	O	U	R	S	B	A

66

Spelling Level 1 Quiz 10

Rearrange these letters to spell out the correct words.

1. e o s o l

2. o l s e

3. s t n o r a y i a t

4. s t n o r e y i a t

5. i n a n t c e

6. e b o u g i r n h

7. r e y e a v y d

8. a w r y

9. y a r e w

10. s n a i c u e n

11. a s v l c e

12. t r e e u t a r m p e

13. t e p a s r i

14. i d u q l i

15. t e s u q

16. e e u u q

17. k i c u q

18. l i l u q

19. c r s i e n e

20. i t v a y r e

Spelling Level 1 Quiz 11

Find the 20 words. They can be found up, down, across or diagonal.

1. leisure
2. programme
3. language
4. alter
5. altar
6. interfere
7. vegetable
8. profession
9. affects
10. effects
11. persuade
12. appearance
13. specific
14. official
15. pension
16. verified
17. secretary
18. equipped
19. attempt
20. reception

B	V	Q	M	P	E	R	S	U	A	D	E	C	I	J	T	X
W	G	P	L	E	I	S	U	R	E	I	R	R	E	P	W	V
D	T	A	H	N	X	F	W	I	N	T	E	R	F	E	R	E
E	O	T	P	E	Q	U	I	P	P	E	D	M	A	J	O	E
Z	S	T	G	V	E	G	E	T	A	B	L	E	L	V	B	W
V	P	E	R	E	C	E	P	T	I	O	N	W	T	Y	M	S
E	E	M	P	R	O	F	E	S	S	I	O	N	E	J	U	P
R	C	P	O	F	F	I	C	I	A	L	G	K	R	R	C	U
I	I	T	K	A	S	D	Q	V	U	J	R	E	O	P	H	X
F	F	K	P	F	A	W	W	C	C	X	H	N	S	E	A	B
I	I	U	R	F	P	R	O	G	R	A	M	M	E	N	M	G
E	C	O	Y	E	L	A	N	G	U	A	G	E	P	S	E	C
D	T	L	Z	C	H	O	E	F	F	E	C	T	S	I	W	W
N	I	G	D	T	D	U	A	L	T	A	R	Z	I	O	O	B
T	X	F	J	S	L	R	S	X	D	O	H	X	E	N	U	O
O	F	M	E	T	C	H	S	E	C	R	E	T	A	R	Y	Z
B	X	E	I	A	P	P	E	A	R	A	N	C	E	R	C	H

Spelling Level 1 Quiz 12

Rearrange these letters to spell out the correct words.

1. i e s u r l e

   l e i s u r e

2. m r p r m g o e a

   p r o g r a m m e

3. n u g g a e l a

   l a n g u a g e

4. l a e t r

   a l t e r

5. l a a t r

   a l t a r

6. r n i r e e t e f

   i n t e r f e r e

7. l e v t b e g e a

   v e g e t a b l e

8. e i n p o f o s r s

   p r o f e s s i o n

9. f s e c t a f

   a f f e c t s

10. f s e c t e f

    e f f e c t s

11. r u d s e e p a

    p e r s u a d e

12. a n e a p e c a p r

    a p p e a r a n c e

13. e i i c p c s f

    s p e c i f i c

14. f c a i f l o i

    o f f i c i a l

15. n n s i o p e

    p e n s i o n

16. r f e i e d v i

    v e r i f i e d

17. r e s e a r c y t

    s e c r e t a r y

18. u p e i q d e p

    e q u i p p e d

19. t t e m p a t

    a t t e m p t

20. o e r p i e c n t

    r e c e p t i o n

69

Spelling Level 1 Quiz 13

Find the 20 words. They can be found up, down, across or diagonal.

1. achieve
2. vehicle
3. equipped
4. business
5. industry
6. temporary
7. hygiene
8. awareness
9. experience
10. security
11. progress
12. receive
13. recognise
14. identify
15. career
16. evidence
17. equipment
18. function
19. physical
20. structure

```
W  P  H  Y  S  I  C  A  L  C  V  U  F  A  P  N  Y  U  I
B  D  V  E  H  I  C  L  E  H  H  M  U  W  R  M  X  U  E
L  E  X  P  E  R  I  E  N  C  E  L  N  A  O  S  Q  P  I
S  T  E  M  P  O  R  A  R  Y  B  M  C  R  G  E  Y  R  A
L  N  C  Q  B  O  M  K  C  U  M  B  T  E  R  S  K  C  K
R  I  G  D  K  M  C  B  D  S  V  V  I  N  E  M  E  Q  A
B  I  D  E  R  V  G  E  U  W  T  I  O  E  S  H  T  B  R
N  A  N  E  M  E  A  F  I  S  T  R  N  S  S  U  X  G  A
H  C  C  D  N  G  C  Q  R  Q  I  A  U  S  I  P  D  B  E
S  H  U  A  U  T  S  O  P  K  Y  N  W  C  V  T  E  G  Q
I  I  W  N  R  S  I  X  G  K  T  A  E  V  T  N  Y  B  U
Z  E  B  J  N  E  T  F  Z  N  K  E  U  S  E  U  F  L  I
V  V  T  E  O  X  E  R  Y  R  I  J  I  I  S  S  R  Q  P
P  E  O  D  W  E  E  R  Y  E  Y  S  G  O  S  C  V  E  M
C  U  Y  J  C  T  G  A  D  C  J  Y  E  N  P  U  E  X  E
S  G  S  B  L  B  S  S  M  E  H  W  E  X  H  A  B  T  N
E  Q  U  I  P  P  E  D  U  I  O  W  T  O  E  X  U  M  T
C  T  O  C  W  B  T  H  P  V  S  E  C  U  R  I  T  Y  Z
V  F  Q  T  G  Z  O  D  S  E  E  V  I  D  E  N  C  E  S
```

70

Spelling Level 1 Quiz 14

Rearrange these letters to spell out the correct words.

1. e h i a v e c

2. e h i v l c e

3. p u e i p q d e

4. e s b i n u s s

5. t d i u s n y r

6. m r e r y t p a o

7. e g i h n e y

8. a s w n s a r e e

9. e i r e e c x p e n

10. i c s u r e y t

11. e o p g r r s s

12. e c e r v i e

13. c s e n e r o i g

14. i e i n t d y f

15. e c e a r r

16. n i e d e v e c

17. u n q m t e i e p

18. i n f c t u n o

19. c y p s i h l a

20. r r t t e s u u c

Spelling Level 1 Quiz 15

💡 Find the 20 words. They can be found up, down, across or diagonal.

1. maintained
2. department
3. workload
4. advise
5. quality
6. research
7. community
8. challenge
9. question
10. soldier
11. evaluate
12. strategy
13. consumer
14. exchange
15. explain
16. survey
17. nominate
18. studio
19. ethics
20. developing

C	C	P	N	J	K	D	E	X	P	L	A	I	N	B	M	W
H	O	Z	K	R	V	B	B	P	X	L	E	T	H	I	C	S
A	N	Y	E	X	C	H	A	N	G	E	Y	O	I	E	T	A
L	S	W	P	S	N	I	P	C	W	O	R	K	L	O	A	D
L	U	M	S	U	R	V	E	Y	N	Q	K	Q	R	D	H	V
E	M	I	T	M	X	Z	E	V	A	L	U	A	T	E	H	V
N	E	J	W	A	I	E	H	L	S	T	U	D	I	O	S	Q
G	R	M	G	D	E	P	A	R	T	M	E	N	T	Z	T	U
E	J	L	K	T	S	C	O	M	M	U	N	I	T	Y	R	A
U	Q	D	Y	Z	T	A	D	V	I	S	E	H	X	I	A	L
C	U	J	K	A	V	R	E	S	E	A	R	C	H	S	T	I
J	E	M	N	O	M	I	N	A	T	E	I	L	O	S	E	T
I	S	X	O	M	A	I	N	T	A	I	N	E	D	H	G	Y
U	T	S	O	L	D	I	E	R	H	G	Z	U	M	A	Y	X
G	I	U	R	L	F	S	M	T	W	Q	D	W	U	J	L	N
K	O	D	C	C	Q	P	F	I	P	X	A	U	A	K	S	F
A	N	B	E	S	Q	B	D	E	V	E	L	O	P	I	N	G

Spelling Level 1 Quiz 16

Rearrange these letters to spell out the correct words.

1. a d m n t a n i e i

2. t t d a r e e m n p

3. o d a r w k l o

4. v e d a s i

5. q u t l i y a

6. e h c s r e a r

7. c m i y u o m n t

8. c l n e l h a e g

9. u n o e q s t i

10. s o e d i r l

11. v e t a e l u a

12. t y g r s a t e

13. o r e n c s u m

14. x e g c e h a n

15. e x i l a n p

16. r y u s e v

17. o e t m n i n a

18. u o t s i d

19. h s t e c i

20. o g d e l e i p n v

THE ANSWERS

Punctuation Level 1 Apostrophe Contraction

Fill in the crossword using an apostrophe where necessary.

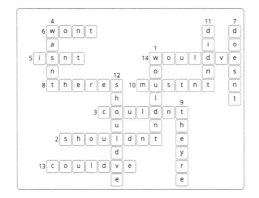

```
        4                              11    7
   6  w  o  n  t              d        d
      a                       i        o
   5  i  s  n  t        1  14 w  o  u  l  d  v  e
      n                    o           n     s
   8  t  h  e  r  e  s  10 m  u  s  t  n  t  n
         h              l              t
                     9
      3  c  o  u  l  d  n  t
         u           n     h
   2  s  h  o  u  l  d  n  t  e
         d           e     y
  13  c  o  u  l  d  v  e     r
         e           e     e
```

Punctuation Level 1 Quiz 1

Identify the Punctuation Marks.

1.

A ☐ QUESTION MARK
B ☒ FULL STOP
C ☐ COMMA

2.

A ☐ APOSTROPHE   B ☐ DASH
C ☒ ELLIPSES

3.

A ☒ COMMA
B ☐ INVERTED COMMAS
C ☐ HYPHEN

4.

A ☐ COLON   B ☒ SEMI-COLON
C ☐ ELLIPSES

5.

A ☐ FULL STOP   B ☐ DASH
C ☒ COLON

6.

A ☒ APOSTROPHE   B ☐ COMMA
C ☐ HYPHEN

Punctuation Level 1 Possessive Apostrophe

How do you show that the subject owns something - Possessive Apostrophe

1.

A ☒ Oliver's cat   B ☐ Oliver' cat
C ☐ Olivers' cat   D ☐ The cat of Oliver

2.

A ☐ the girl's bag   B ☒ the girls' bags
C ☐ the girl's bags   D ☐ The bags of the girls

3.

A ☐ Luigis' bus   B ☐ Luigi bus
C ☒ Luigi's bus   D ☐ The bus of luigi

4.

A ☒ the boys' books
B ☐ the boy's book
C ☐ the boy's books
D ☐ The books of the boys

5.

A ☐ Mr Browns hat   B ☒ Mr Brown's hat
C ☐ Mr Browns' hat   D ☐ The hat of Mr Brown

6.

A ☐ Rosys' bike   B ☐ Rosy' bike
C ☒ Rosy's bike   D ☐ The bike of Rosy

7.

A ☐ the twin's hats   B ☒ the twins' hats
C ☐ the twin hats   D ☐ the hats of the twins

7.

A ☐ QUESTION MARK
B ☒ HYPHEN
C ☐ DASH

8.

A ☒ INVERTED COMMAS
B ☐ COMMA
C ☐ QUESTION MARK

9.

A ☐ EXCLAMATION MARK
B ☐ FULL STOP
C ☒ QUESTION MARK

10.
!

A ☐ SEMI-COLON
B ☒ EXCLAMATION MARK
C ☐ APOSTROPHE

11.
( )

A ☒ BRACKETS   B ☐ ELLIPSES
C ☐ COLON

12.
―――

A ☐ HYPHEN   B ☒ DASH
C ☐ FULL STOP

74

Punctuation Level 1 Quiz 2

💡 How do you use Punctuation?

1. what do you use before but and because?
   - A ☐ apostrophe
   - B ☐ full stop
   - C ☒ comma
   - D ☐ question mark

2. when do you use a apostrophe?
   - A ☐ ending a sentence
   - B ☐ replacing a conjunction
   - C ☐ sentence starters
   - D ☒ replacing a letter don't can't

3. what do you use a semicolon for?
   - A ☒ replacing a conjunction
   - B ☐ starting a list
   - C ☐ starting or ending speech
   - D ☐ separating a sentence

4. what do you put when you start a list?
   - A ☐ apostrophe
   - B ☒ colon
   - C ☐ semicolon
   - D ☐ comma

5. what do you use a question mark for?
   - A ☐ being angry at someone
   - B ☒ asking a question
   - C ☐ replacing a conjunction
   - D ☐ starting a list

6. when do you use an exclamation mark?
   - A ☐ separating a sentence
   - B ☐ ending a sentence
   - C ☒ when you are yelling at someone
   - D ☐ replacing a conjunction

7. what do you put at the end of a sentence?
   - A ☐ comma
   - B ☐ semicolon
   - C ☐ question mark
   - D ☒ full stop

8. what do you sometimes use at a end of a paragraph?
   - A ☒ ellipsis
   - B ☐ exclamation mark
   - C ☐ apostrophe
   - D ☐ colon

9. What do you use to show someone is speaking directly?
   - A ☒ 66 99 quotation marks
   - B ☐ ? question mark
   - C ☐ ! exclamation mark
   - D ☐ ; two commas

10. What should go at the end of this sentence?
   - A ☐ exclamation mark
   - B ☐ full stop
   - C ☒ question mark
   - D ☐ comma

11. How would you show that I'm shouting a sentence?
   - A ☐ question mark
   - B ☐ elipses
   - C ☒ exclamation mark
   - D ☐ full stop

12. What do I use to abbreviate (shorten) the word cannot?
   - A ☐ comma
   - B ☐ quotation marks
   - C ☐ apostrophe
   - D ☐ semi colon

13. What do I use before writing a list?
   - A ☐ semi colon
   - B ☒ colon
   - C ☐ comma
   - D ☐ full stop

14. Every sentence starts with...
   - A ☐ a full stop
   - B ☐ a quotation mark
   - C ☐ a comma
   - D ☒ a capital letter

15. Which of the following needs a capital letter?
   - A ☐ school
   - B ☐ home
   - C ☒ paris
   - D ☐ church

16. Which of the following needs a capital letter?
   - A ☒ st mary's church
   - B ☐ my home
   - C ☐ my house
   - D ☐ my street

What event did Joey attend on Saturday? THE FOOTBALL GAME

How did Joey show his support for his team? HE WORE HIS FAVOURITE TEAM SHIRT

What was the atmosphere like at the stadium? IT BUZZED WITH EXCITEMENT

What happened during the game that made Joey's heart race? HIS TEAM SCORED A GOAL

How did Joey feel at the end of the game? HE FELT JUBILATION

Where did Carly visit on Sunday? SHE WENT TO A ZOO

What did Carly bring with her to the zoo? HER CAMERA

Which animals did Carly encounter during her visit? LIONS

How did Carly describe the lions at the zoo? THEY WERE MAJESTIC

What unique experience did Carly have with the giraffes? SHE GOT TO FEED THE GIRAFFES

Punctuation Level 1 Quiz 3

Draw a line to match the Punctuation Marks to their definition.

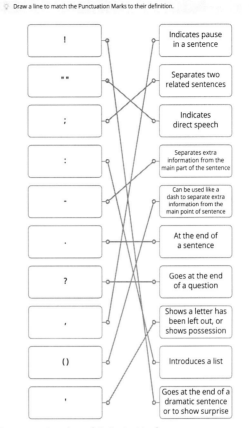

!	Indicates pause in a sentence
" "	Separates two related sentences
;	Indicates direct speech
:	Separates extra information from the main part of the sentence
-	Can be used like a dash to separate extra information from the main point of sentence
.	At the end of a sentence
?	Goes at the end of a question
,	Shows a letter has been left out, or shows possession
( )	Introduces a list
'	Goes at the end of a dramatic sentence or to show surprise

Punctuation Level 1 Quiz Airplane

Draw a path from each airplane to its answer - don't crash into other clouds along the way

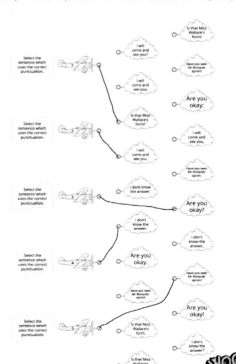

Select the sentence which uses the correct punctuation.

Purpose of Text Level 1 Quiz 4

Read the text, then try and match up what each section is talking about.

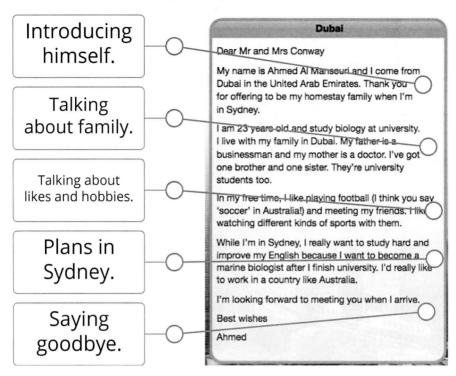

Introducing himself.

Talking about family.

Talking about likes and hobbies.

Plans in Sydney.

Saying goodbye.

Dubai

Dear Mr and Mrs Conway

My name is Ahmed Al Mansouri and I come from Dubai in the United Arab Emirates. Thank you for offering to be my homestay family when I'm in Sydney.

I am 23 years old and study biology at university. I live with my family in Dubai. My father is a businessman and my mother is a doctor. I've got one brother and one sister. They're university students too.

In my free time, I like playing football (I think you say 'soccer' in Australia!) and meeting my friends. I like watching different kinds of sports with them.

While I'm in Sydney, I really want to study hard and improve my English because I want to become a marine biologist after I finish university. I'd really like to work in a country like Australia.

I'm looking forward to meeting you when I arrive.

Best wishes

Ahmed

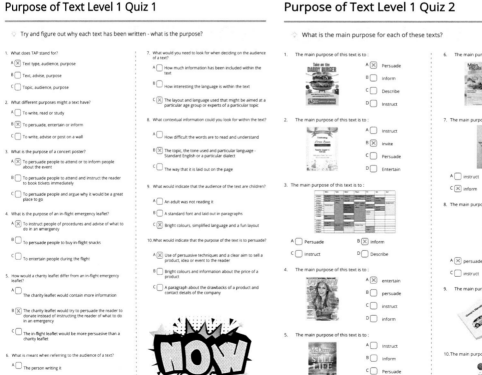

Purpose of Text Level 1 Quiz 1

Try and figure out why each text has been written - what is the purpose?

1. What does TAP stand for?
   - A ☒ Text type, audience, purpose
   - B ☐ Text, advise, purpose
   - C ☐ Topic, audience, purpose

2. What different purposes might a text have?
   - A ☐ To write, read or study
   - B ☒ To persuade, entertain or inform
   - C ☐ To write, advise or post on a wall

3. What is the purpose of a concert poster?
   - A ☒ To persuade people to attend or to inform people about the event
   - B ☐ To persuade people to attend and instruct the reader to book tickets immediately
   - C ☐ To persuade people and argue why it would be a great place to go

4. What is the purpose of an in-flight emergency leaflet?
   - A ☒ To instruct people of procedures and advise of what to do in an emergency
   - B ☐ To persuade people to buy in-flight snacks
   - C ☐ To entertain people during the flight

5. How would a charity leaflet differ from an in-flight emergency leaflet?
   - A ☐ The charity leaflet would contain more information
   - B ☒ The charity leaflet would try to persuade the reader to donate instead of instructing the reader of what to do in an emergency
   - C ☐ The in-flight leaflet would be more persuasive than a charity leaflet

6. What is meant when referring to the audience of a text?
   - A ☐ The person writing it
   - B ☒ The particular group of people that the text was aimed at when written
   - C ☐ The people viewing the text if it is displayed

7. What would you need to look for when deciding on the audience of a text?
   - A ☐ How much information has been included within the text
   - B ☐ How interesting the language is within the text
   - C ☒ The layout and language used that might be aimed at a particular age group or experts of a particular topic

8. What contextual information could you look for within the text?
   - A ☐ How difficult the words are to read and understand
   - B ☒ The topic, the tone used and particular language - Standard English or a particular dialect
   - C ☐ The way that it is laid out on the page

9. What would indicate that the audience of the text are children?
   - A ☐ An adult was not reading it
   - B ☐ A standard font and laid out in paragraphs
   - C ☒ Bright colours, simplified language and a fun layout

10. What would indicate that the purpose of the text is to persuade?
    - A ☒ Use of persuasive techniques and a clear aim to sell a product, idea or event to the reader
    - B ☐ Bright colours and information about the price of a product
    - C ☐ A paragraph about the drawbacks of a product and contact details of the company

Purpose of Text Level 1 Quiz 2

What is the main purpose for each of these texts?

1. The main purpose of this text is to :
   - A ☒ Persuade
   - B ☐ Inform
   - C ☐ Describe
   - D ☐ Instruct

2. The main purpose of this text is to :
   - A ☐ Instruct
   - B ☒ Invite
   - C ☐ Persuade
   - D ☐ Entertain

3. The main purpose of this text is to :
   - A ☐ Persuade
   - B ☒ Inform
   - C ☐ Instruct
   - D ☐ Describe

4. The main purpose of this text is to :
   - A ☒ entertain
   - B ☐ persuade
   - C ☐ instruct
   - D ☐ inform

5. The main purpose of this text is to :
   - A ☐ Instruct
   - B ☐ Inform
   - C ☐ Persuade
   - D ☒ Entertain

6. The main purpose of this text is to :
   - A ☒ Instruct
   - B ☐ Persuade
   - C ☐ inform
   - D ☐ entertain

7. The main purpose of this text is to :
   - A ☐ instruct
   - B ☐ entertain
   - C ☒ inform
   - D ☐ persuade

8. The main purpose of this text is to :
   - A ☒ persuade
   - B ☐ inform
   - C ☐ instruct
   - D ☐ entertain

9. The main purpose of this text is to :
   - A ☐ inform
   - B ☐ persuade
   - C ☒ instruct
   - D ☐ describe

10. The main purpose of this text is to :
    - A ☐ advise
    - B ☐ persuade
    - C ☐ entertain
    - D ☒ inform

Purpose of Text Level 1 Quiz 3

Rearrange these letters to spell out the correct Purpose of Text.

1. A leaflet about a theme park
M O R F N I
`I` `N` `F` `O` `R` `M`

2. Assembly details for Ikea Furniture
T N S I C R U T
`I` `N` `S` `T` `R` `U` `C` `T`

3. An advert in a newspaper
E E R P D U A S
`P` `E` `R` `S` `U` `A` `D` `E`

4. A web page telling how to save money
E I S V D A
`A` `D` `V` `I` `S` `E`

5. A report giving both sides of an argument
S S D S I U C
`D` `I` `S` `C` `U` `S` `S`

6. A letter protesting dog walking on public beaches
U G E R A
`A` `R` `G` `U` `E`

7. A recipe for making apple pie
T N S I C R U T
`I` `N` `S` `T` `R` `U` `C` `T`

8. If you want to get your point across
U G E R A
`A` `R` `G` `U` `E`

9. Trying to get someone to agree with you
E F R P D U A S
`P` `E` `R` `S` `U` `A` `D` `E`

10. A notice next to a fire extinguisher
T N S I C R U T
`I` `N` `S` `T` `R` `U` `C` `T`

Purpose of Text Level 1 Quiz 5

Write in the box provided the purpose of each text from the words listed below.

1. Turn left at the end of the roadGo as far as the traffic lightsTurn rightMy house is the first one on the left after the shop
INSTRUCT

2. Give water Give lifeGive £2 a month
PERSUADE

3. Great news for people aged 50 and over! Low cost Home and Motor Insurance
PERSUADE

4. This year there has been a lot of flooding due to the high rainfall. Lots of people have had their homes spoiled by flood water
INFORM

5. Your motor insurance is due for renewal
INFORM

6. Melt the butter and sugarMix in the flourBeat in the eggsAdd to the mixture
INSTRUCT

7. You can't afford to miss this offer!
PERSUADE

8. This garment must be dry cleaned
INSTRUCT

9. Palace Theatre Monday 13th June 7.30 pmJunior ShowtimeStalls D13
INFORM

10. The sky was so clear and blue. The wind whistled around my ears.
DESCRIBE

11. Ten students are in my ESOL class. They are Polish, Romanian, Pakistani and Spanish. The class is quite small and friendly.
DESCRIBE

Purpose of Text Level 1 Quiz Airplane

Draw a path from each airplane to its answer - don't crash into other clouds along the way

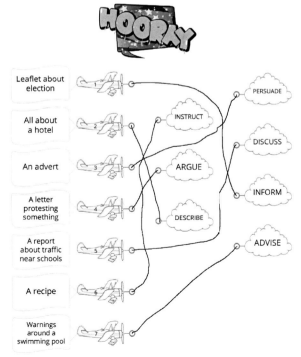

Leaflet about election

All about a hotel

An advert

A letter protesting something

A report about traffic near schools

A recipe

Warnings around a swimming pool

PERSUADE · INSTRUCT · DISCUSS · ARGUE · INFORM · DESCRIBE · ADVISE

Grammar Level 1 Quiz 1

Look at the Spelling, Punctuation and Grammar before you choose a correct sentence.

1. Which sentence is correct?
   A ☐ Taylors dog's are very noisy.
   B ☒ Taylor's dogs are very noisy.

2. Which sentence is correct?
   A ☒ We should have come earlier.
   B ☐ We should of come earlier.

3. Which sentence uses Standard English?
   A ☐ We was all really excited about our holiday.
   B ☐ We is all really excited about our holiday.
   C ☒ We are all really excited about our holiday.

4. Which sentence uses Standard English?
   A ☒ I did my homework last night.
   B ☐ I done my homework last night.

5. My Auntie Sue lives alone. With this in mind, which sentence is punctuated correctly?
   A ☐ I am going to my aunties house later.
   B ☒ I am going to my auntie's house later.
   C ☐ I am going to my aunties' house later.

6. Which sentence has the correct use of inverted commas for direct speech?
   A ☒ "Will you come to my party?" Sophie asked me.
   B ☐ "Will you come to my party"? Sophie asked me.
   C ☐ "Will you come to my party? Sophie asked me."

Grammar Level 1 Quiz 2

Put a check under each mole that should start with a capital letter

Row 1: cities ✓ | animals | names ✓ | seasons ✓

Row 2: road names ✓ | birthday | months of the year ✓ | personal pronoun 'i' ✓

Row 3: book titles ✓ | plants | days of week ✓ | common nouns

Row 4: adverbs | verbs | rivers and oceans ✓ | food ✓

Row 5: countries ✓ | adjectives

Grammar Level 1 Quiz 4

Keep on Going! Know your Grammar!

1. Click on the correct word to complete the sentence. We were _____ on our topics.

   A ☐ worked   B ☐ works
   C ☒ working   D ☐ work

2. Click on the correct word to complete the sentence in the **past tense**. I _____ to Scotland during the school holidays.

   A ☐ go   B ☐ going
   C ☒ went   D ☐ was

3. Click on the correct word to complete the sentence. Tomorrow, we could go for a walk _____ play games indoors.

   A ☐ when   B ☒ or
   C ☐ because   D ☐ if

4. Click on the correct word to complete the sentence. _____ you go to the park, you can play a game.

   A ☐ And   B ☐ So
   C ☐ But   D ☒ If

5. Which sentence is a **command**?

   A ☒ Pack away your paints now.
   B ☐ You should be proud of your work.
   C ☐ Will you show me your painting?
   D ☐ That's your best work yet!

6. Choose the correct suffix to add to the word **fall** in this sentence. The autumn leaves are fall___ to the ground.

   A ☐ ed   B ☐ s
   C ☐ est   D ☒ ing

7. Choose a suffix to add to the word **fast** in this sentence. The hare knew that he could run fast___ than the tortoise.

   A ☒ er   B ☐ est
   C ☐ ing   D ☐ ed

8. What type of word is in bold in this sentence? Gran thought the flowers were **pretty**.

   A ☐ noun   B ☐ verb
   C ☒ adjective   D ☐ adverb

9. Why do the bold words start with a capital letter? On **Saturday** morning, **Sarah** and her family went on holiday to **Scotland**.

   A ☐ They are nouns   B ☒ they are proper nouns
   C ☐ they are adjectives   D ☐ at the beginning of a sentence.

10. How many nouns are in this sentence? **You have left your pencil on the bench over there.**

    A ☐ 1   B ☒ 2
    C ☐ 3   D ☐ 4

11. What type of sentence is this? **One day, Ali decided to make a toy robot.**

    A ☐ a question   B ☒ a statement
    C ☐ a command   D ☐ an exclamation

12. Click on the word which is an adverb in this sentence. **jamie knocked softly on his brother's bedroom door.**

    A ☐ knocked   B ☐ door
    C ☒ softly   D ☐ brother

13. Which sentence uses an apostrophe correctly?

    A ☒ Lucy's bag is green and has lots of pockets.
    B ☐ Lucys' bag is green and has lots of pockets.
    C ☐ Lucys bag is green and has lot's of pockets.
    D ☐ Lucys bag is green and has lots of pocket's.

14. Which sentence uses a comma correctly?

    A ☐ The museum shop sell,s posters mugs and badges.
    B ☐ The museum, shop sells posters mugs an badges.
    C ☐ The museum shop sells posters mugs, and badges.
    D ☒ The museum shop sells posters, mugs and badges.

15. Which punctuation mark completes the sentence? **What a wonderful present you gave me**

    A ☐ full stop   B ☒ exclamation mark
    C ☐ question mark   D ☐ comma

Grammar Level 1 Quiz 3

Test your Grammar Skills!

1. Which kind of punctuation mark would complete the sentence? Can we go to the cinema please

   A ☐ !   B ☐ .
   C ☐ ,   D ☒ ?

2. Which word completes the sentence? We_____ our bikes.

   A ☐ rided   B ☐ rides
   C ☐ riding   D ☒ rode

3. look at the words. Which needs an **es** to make it into a plural?

   A ☐ pencil   B ☒ fox
   C ☐ dog   D ☐ chair

4. Which sentence is a **statement**?

   A ☐ What time is the bus due to arrive?
   B ☒ I rode my bike to school.
   C ☐ What an enormous aeroplane!
   D ☐ Bring your scooter when you come to play.

5. Which sentence is a command?

   A ☐ What time does the pool open?
   B ☒ Bring your swimming costume to the pool.
   C ☐ What an amazing swim!
   D ☐ I am learning to swim.

6. Click on the verb in this sentence. Lottie was jumping really high on the trampoline.

   A ☐ trampoline
   B ☐ high
   C ☒ was
   D ☐ really

7. Which sentence is in the past tense?

   A ☒ Tom rode his bike.
   B ☐ Daniel is running.
   C ☐ Rebecca will read her book.
   D ☐ Joe is writing.

8. What word is the contracted form of **could have**?

   A ☐ could'ave   B ☐ coul've
   C ☒ could've   D ☐ could ve

Grammar Level 1 Quiz 5

It's a tricky one! Unjumble the words and rearrange them to make a proper sentence.

1. i s   r o y u   d a d
   w g r n k i o   n w o ?

   | I s | | your |
   | d a d |
   | w o r k i n g |
   | n o w ? |

2. e A r   y o u   n a c t h i g w
   N x t i f l e ?

   | A r e | y o u |
   | w a t c h i n g |
   | N e t f l i x ? |

3. e A r   t h e   i r g s l
   d g n n c i a ?

   | A r e | t h e |
   | g i r l s |
   | d a n c i n g ? |

4. i s   t R e o b r
   g s i i n l n t e   o t
   s i c u m ?

   | I s | R o b e r t |
   | l i s t e n i n g |
   | t o | m u s i c ? |

5. i s   t h e   d o g
   r g n n n i u ?

   | I s | t h e |
   | d o g |
   | r u n n i n g ? |

6. e A r   S a m   a n d   T m o
   s i n g n g i ?

   | A r e | S a m |
   | a n d | T o m |
   | s i n g i n g ? |

7. i s   o u r   c a t
   l n i s e e p g ?

   | I s | o u r |
   | c a t |
   | s l e e p i n g ? |

8. e A r   y h t e
   n w m i m i g s   n i   t e h
   s e a ?

   | A r e | t h e y |
   | s w i m m i n g |
   | i n | t h e |
   | s e a ? |

9. i s   L e a   n h t a t i g c
   o t   h r e   a t e e r c h ?

   | I s | L e a |
   | c h a t t i n g |
   | t o | h e r |
   | t e a c h e r ? |

Grammar Level 1 Quiz 6

Here's a few more SPAG questions.

1. Click on the correct word to complete the sentence. **We were_____ on our topics.**
   - A ☐ worked
   - B ☐ works
   - C ☒ working
   - D ☐ work

2. Click on the correct word to complete the sentence in the past tense. **I _____ to Scotland during the school holidays.**
   - A ☐ go
   - B ☐ going
   - C ☒ went
   - D ☐ was

3. Click on the correct word to complete the sentence. **Tomorrow, we could go for a walk _____ play games indoors.**
   - A ☐ when
   - B ☒ or
   - C ☐ because
   - D ☐ if

4. Click on the correct word to complete the sentence. **_____ you go to the park, you can play a game.**
   - A ☐ And
   - B ☐ So
   - C ☐ But
   - D ☒ If

5. Which sentence is a command?
   - A ☒ Pack away your paints now.
   - B ☐ You should be proud of your work.
   - C ☐ Will you show me your painting?
   - D ☐ That's your best work yet!

6. Choose the correct suffix to add to the word fall in this sentence. **The autumn leaves are fall___ to the ground.**
   - A ☐ ed
   - B ☐ s
   - C ☐ est
   - D ☒ ing

7. Choose a suffix to add to the word fast in this sentence. **The hare knew that he could run fast___ than the tortoise.**
   - A ☒ er
   - B ☐ est
   - C ☐ ing
   - D ☐ ed

8. What type of word is in **bold** in this sentence? "Gran thought the flowers were **pretty.**"
   - A ☐ noun
   - B ☐ verb
   - C ☒ adjective
   - D ☐ adverb

9. In this sentence, why does Saturday, Sarah and Scotland have a capital letter? On **Saturday** morning, **Sarah** and her family went on holiday to **Scotland.**
   - A ☐ They are nouns
   - B ☒ they are proper nouns
   - C ☐ they are adjectives
   - D ☐ at the beginning of a sentence.

10. How many nouns are in this sentence? **You have left your pencil on the bench over there.**
    - A ☐ 1
    - B ☒ 2
    - C ☐ 3
    - D ☐ 4

11. What type of sentence is this? **One day, Ali decided to make a toy robot.**
    - A ☐ a question
    - B ☒ a statement
    - C ☐ a command
    - D ☐ an exclamation

12. Which word is an adverb in this sentence? **Jamie knocked softly on his brother's bedroom door.**
    - A ☐ knocked
    - B ☐ door
    - C ☒ softly
    - D ☐ brother

13. Which sentence uses an apostrophe correctly?
    - A ☒ Lucy's bag is green and has lots of pockets.
    - B ☐ Lucys' bag is green and has lots of pockets.
    - C ☐ Lucys bag is green and has lot's of pockets.
    - D ☐ Lucys bag is green and has lots of pocket's.

14. Which sentence uses a comma correctly?
    - A ☐ The museum shop sell,s posters mugs and badges.
    - B ☐ The museum, shop sells posters mugs an badges.
    - C ☐ The museum shop sells posters mugs, and badges.
    - D ☒ The museum shop sells posters, mugs and badges.

15. Which punctuation mark completes the sentence? **What a wonderful present you gave me**
    - A ☐ full stop
    - B ☒ exclamation mark
    - C ☐ question mark
    - D ☐ comma

Sentence Level 1 Quiz 1

Only one sentence is correct. See if you can find which is most grammatically correct.

1. She doesn't
   - A ☐ to the doctor go
   - B ☒ go to the doctor
   - C ☐ the doctor go

2. I like
   - A ☒ it because it's healthy
   - B ☐ because healthy
   - C ☐ because healthy is

3. Next week
   - A ☐ to Newport I'll go
   - B ☐ I'll to Newport go
   - C ☒ I'll go to Newport

4. I want
   - A ☐ job doctor
   - B ☐ future job doctor
   - C ☒ to be a doctor

5. My daughter
   - A ☒ wants to go to school
   - B ☐ wants school
   - C ☐ want go school

6. Jasmin says
   - A ☐ she went to the zoo tomorrow
   - B ☒ she went to the zoo yesterday
   - C ☐ she may go to the zoo last week
   - D ☐ she will definitely go to the zoo last Friday

7. Yanni needs to go and buy
   - A ☐ summet for tea
   - B ☐ some groceries yesterday
   - C ☒ some: milk, bread, and cheese

8. If you work hard in college
   - A ☐ there are lots of nice people there
   - B ☐ there is a great cafe
   - C ☒ you will learn a lot

9. He needs three shirts
   - A ☐ so he will bought some next week
   - B ☐ so he will brought them from a shop
   - C ☒ so he will need to save up some money

10. She gave a
    - A ☐ through account of her actions
    - B ☐ though account of her actions
    - C ☒ thorough account of her actions

Organisational Features Level 1 Quiz 1

Can you match up the organisational features?

1. Small symbols, often black circles, used to list items
2. A box with a border (separate from the main text)
3. Additional information at the bottom of the page
4. A box with rows and columns (containing information)
5. Words which are darker/heavier
6. Inform the reader what the text is about

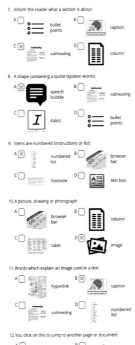

7. Inform the reader what a section is about
8. A shape containing a quote (spoken words)
9. Items are numbered (instructions or list)
10. A picture, drawing or photograph
11. Words which explain an image used in a text
12. You click on this to jump to another page or document

Letter L1 Quiz 1

Draw a line from each of the elements of the letter to the position they should go.

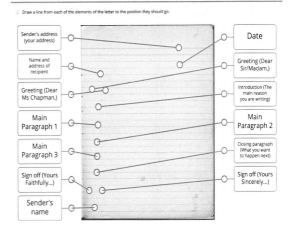

Email Level 1 Quiz 1

Draw a line from each of the elements of an email to the correct position they should be on the email.

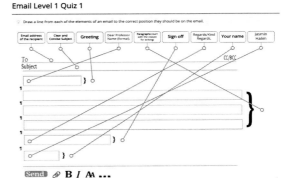

Sentence Level 1 Quiz 2

Write in the item numbers of the correct and incorrect sentences. Especially look how each sentence starts and how it ends.

Correct: 1 7 9 15 3 8 14 □

Incorrect: 2 5 10 12 4 6 11 13

1	2	3	4	5
The elephants needed help because they were hurt.	the selfish baboon kept all the coconuts.	After that, the happy giant smiled and gave Jack his golden egg.	Last night, the dog .	Soon, the.

6	7	8	9	10
After that, the happy giant smiled and gave egg	Suddenly, the elephants needed help.	Soon, the elephants were charging at me.	Last night, the dog barked loudly.	Last night, the dog barked loudly

11	12	13	14	15
Elephants needed help came	The were charging at me.	the elephants needed help because they were hurt	Suddenly, the elephants needed help but no-one came.	Next, the baboon kept all the coconuts because he was greedy.

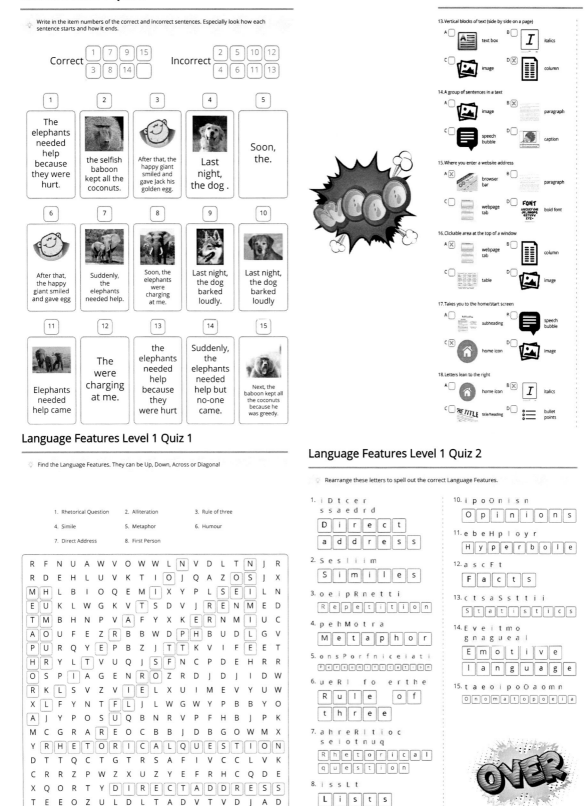

13. Vertical blocks of text (side by side on a page)
- A □ text box
- B □ italics
- C □ image
- D ☒ column

14. A group of sentences in a text
- A ☒ image
- B ☒ paragraph
- C □ speech bubble
- D □ caption

15. Where you enter a website address
- A ☒ browser bar
- B □ paragraph
- C □ webpage tab
- D □ bold font

16. Clickable area at the top of a window
- A ☒ webpage tab
- B □ column
- C □ table
- D □ image

17. Takes you to the home/start screen
- A □ subheading
- B □ speech bubble
- C ☒ home icon
- D □ image

18. Letters lean to the right
- A □ home icon
- B ☒ italics
- C □ title/heading
- D □ bullet points

Language Features Level 1 Quiz 1

Find the Language Features. They can be Up, Down, Across or Diagonal

1. Rhetorical Question 2. Alliteration 3. Rule of three
4. Simile 5. Metaphor 6. Humour
7. Direct Address 8. First Person

```
R F N U A W V O W W L N V D L T N J R
R D E H L U V K T I O J Q A Z O S J X
M H L B I O Q E M I X Y P L S E I L N
E U K L W G K V T S D V J R E N M E D
T M B H N P V A F Y X K E R N M I U C
A O U F E Z R B B W D P H B U D L G V
P U R Q Y E P B Z J T T K V I F E E T
H R Y L T V U Q J S F N C P D E H R R
O S P I A G E N R O Z R D J D J I D W
R K L S V Z V I E L X U I M E V Y U W
X L F Y N T F L J L W G W Y P B B Y O
A J Y P O S U Q B N R V P F H B J P K
M C G R A R E O C B B J D B G O W M X
Y R H E T O R I C A L Q U E S T I O N
D T T Q C T G T R S A F I V C C L V K
C R R Z P W Z X U Z Y E F R H C Q D E
X Q O R T Y D I R E C T A D D R E S S
T E E O Z U L D L T A D V T V D J A D
Z I N M M R Y E N B R Y U F O C A R Y
```

Language Features Level 1 Quiz 2

Rearrange these letters to spell out the correct Language Features.

1. i D t c e r s s a e d r d — D i r e c t a d d r e s s
2. S e s l i i m — S i m i l e s
3. o e i p R n e t t i — R e p e t i t i o n
4. p e h M o t r a — M e t a p h o r
5. o n s P o r f n i c e i a t i — P e r s o n i f i c a t i o n
6. u e R l f o e r t h e — R u l e o f t h r e e
7. a h r e R l t i o c s e i o t n u q — R h e t o r i c a l q u e s t i o n
8. i s s L t — L i s t s
9. e n i l o a t A t r i l — A l l i t e r a t i o n
10. i p o O n i s n — O p i n i o n s
11. e b e H p l o y r — H y p e r b o l e
12. a s c F t — F a c t s
13. c t s a S s t t i i — S t a t i s t i c s
14. E v e i t m o g n a u g e a l — E m o t i v e l a n g u a g e
15. t a e o i p o O a o m n — O n o m a t o p o e i a

These answers are only suggestions. You have probably come up with different, but still correct answers.

SLANG/Very Informal	INFORMAL/normal	FORMAL
Piddly	very small	insignificant
Chuffed	pleased	delighted
Bevy	drink	beverage
Specs	glasses	spectacles
Bloke	man	gentleman
Ace	great	brilliant
Mate	friend	acquaintance
Pick your brains	ask	enquire
Shut up	be quiet	refrain from conversation
Kid	child	adolescent
Digs	house	residence
Hi	hello	salutations
See Ya!	goodbye	farewell

Language Features Level 1 Quiz 3

Draw a line to match the definition with the Language Feature

Direct address	3 describing words in a list
Triple/list of 3/ rule of 3	A question that doesn't need an answer
Simile	Sound effect words
Onomatopoeia	Describes how something is
Rhetorical question	A doing word
Adjective	Comparison using LIKE or AS
Hyperbole	Saying something IS something that it can't literally be
Alliteration	Talking at the reader using 'you'
Metaphor	3 (or more) words in a sentence with the same starting letter
Personification	Giving a non-human human qualities
Adverb	Over-exaggeration for effect
Verb	Describes how something is done

Formal v Informal Level 1 Quiz 4

Only put a check under the INFORMAL moles

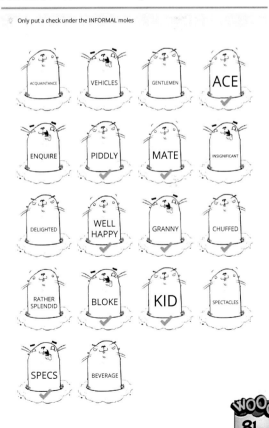

ACQUAINTANCE VEHICLES GENTLEMEN ACE ✓

ENQUIRE PIDDLY ✓ MATE ✓ INSIGNIFICANT

DELIGHTED WELL HAPPY ✓ GRANNY ✓ CHUFFED ✓

RATHER SPLENDID BLOKE ✓ KID ✓ SPECTACLES

SPECS ✓ BEVERAGE

woooooo 81

Formal v Informal Level 1 Quiz 2

Write in the item numbers in the list of boxes for each group

Formal ⟨2⟩⟨5⟩⟨6⟩⟨7⟩⟨14⟩⟨17⟩⟨18⟩⟨19⟩⟨20⟩⟨21⟩⟨22⟩⟨23⟩

Informal ⟨1⟩⟨3⟩⟨4⟩⟨8⟩⟨9⟩⟨10⟩⟨11⟩⟨12⟩⟨13⟩⟨15⟩⟨16⟩

1	2	3	4
See you soon.	With reference to your letter dated ...	I want to know about ...	Thanks for your letter.

5	6	7	8
I am writing to express my concerns.	Yours sincerely,	Yours faithfully,	Best wishes,

9	10	11	12
Lots of love.	Hi!	Dear Nanny and Grandad,	I got your letter.

13	14	15	16
Let me know if it's OK.	Please find enclosed ...	Give my love to ...	I'm writing to tell you that ...

17	18	19	20
To whom it may concern.	I look forward to hearing from you.	Dear Sir or Madam,	I would like to confirm that ...

21	22	23
I am writing to apply for the position of ...	Please contact me if you require any further information.	Dear Mrs Smith,

Formal v Informal Level 1 Quiz 3

Choose the most appropriate answer for formal writing

1. In a formal letter, you will always write to someone you know
   A ☐ True   B ☒ False

2. What tone should a formal letter always have?
   A ☐ forceful   B ☒ appropriate and polite   C ☐ patronising

3. If you do not know the recipient's name, your formal letter should always end
   A ☐ Yours sincerely   B ☐ Yours with love   C ☒ Yours faithfully

4. Your formal letter should always include
   A ☐ a long opening paragraph
   B ☒ a brief opening paragraph which introduces your reason for writing
   C ☐ bullet points with the main reasons for writing

5. The person you are writing to
   A ☐ purpose   B ☐ content
   C ☒ audience   D ☐ format

6. The reason you are writing a formal letter
   A ☒ purpose   B ☐ content
   C ☐ audience   D ☐ format

7. The layout of a formal letter
   A ☐ purpose   B ☐ content
   C ☐ audience   D ☒ format

8. The topic of your letter
   A ☐ purpose   B ☒ content
   C ☐ audience   D ☐ format

Fact v Opinion Level 1 Quiz 1

Write in the item numbers in the list of boxes for each group

Fact ⟨1⟩⟨4⟩⟨5⟩⟨6⟩⟨10⟩⟨12⟩⟨14⟩⟨16⟩⟨17⟩⟨18⟩

Opinion ⟨2⟩⟨3⟩⟨7⟩⟨8⟩⟨9⟩⟨11⟩⟨13⟩⟨15⟩⟨19⟩⟨20⟩

1	2	3	4
The UK Prime Minister lives in Downing Street	10 Downing Street is better than the Whitehouse	English is boring	The BBC is funded by a licence fee

5	6	7	8
London is the capital of England	King Charles' mother was the Queen	Workers in the UK pay too much income tax	Manchester should be the capital of England

9	10	11	12
Facebook is better than X	Paris is the capital of France	The British are the most polite of all people	Donald Trump was the President

13	14	15	16
The BBC is biased	Apples and Oranges are fruit	Donald Trump was the best President	Workers in the UK pay income tax

17	18	19	20
There are 7 days in a week	Twitter is now called X	Apples are better than Oranges	King Charles is a better leader than the Queen

Fact v Opinion Level 1 Quiz 2

Match the statements to whether they are FACT or OPINION

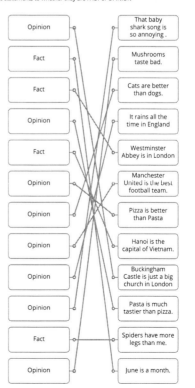

Left column: Opinion, Fact, Fact, Opinion, Fact, Opinion, Opinion, Opinion, Opinion, Opinion, Fact, Opinion

Right column: That baby shark song is so annoying . / Mushrooms taste bad. / Cats are better than dogs. / It rains all the time in England / Westminster Abbey is in London / Manchester United is the best football team. / Pizza is better than Pasta / Hanoi is the capital of Vietnam. / Buckingham Castle is just a big church in London / Pasta is much tastier than pizza. / Spiders have more legs than me. / June is a month.

Fact v Opinion Level 1 Quiz 3

Put a check below each of the moles that have a FACT.

(Moles grid with captions:)
- Boston is famous for the pilgrims
- Leeds has a University ✓
- Cabbage is Horrible
- Climate change is real
- Miami has the best beach
- Too many people live in Manchester
- The Earth is roundish ✓
- TV's future is bleak
- Florida has sandy beaches ✓
- Some people like jazz music ✓
- Teens are watching less traditional television
- The Earth is overpopulated
- Broadcast TV is losing viewers
- Cabbage can be Green ✓
- Teens should watch less television
- Everyone should love brass bands
- Leeds University is brilliant
- Boston is officially boring
- Save the planet today, or we're all going to die
- Manchester is a City ✓

Spelling Level 1 Quiz 1

Find the 20 words. They can be found up, down, across or diagonal.

1. principal 2. principle 3. apparent 4. occupy 5. draft
6. draught 7. prophet 8. profit 9. feet 10. feat
11. familiar 12. heard 13. herd 14. amateur 15. twelfth
16. yacht 17. particular 18. conscious 19. embarrass 20. suggest

S	A	S	C	W	P	F	E	E	T	K	Y	A	C	H	T
P	A	R	T	I	C	U	L	A	R	J	O	A	O	R	C
P	E	F	E	D	R	A	U	G	H	T	Y	D	Y	A	E
R	P	R	I	N	C	I	P	A	L	J	R	L	N	T	H
I	F	G	A	Z	F	B	E	K	A	E	J	E	I	T	H
N	Q	E	D	Q	A	C	M	D	H	W	S	F	F	P	I
C	U	O	A	H	P	O	B	G	S	I	O	L	B	J	C
I	H	W	B	T	A	N	A	S	S	R	E	I	H	F	D
P	S	H	A	N	P	S	R	U	P	W	D	X	E	L	R
L	H	L	M	P	P	C	R	G	T	R	G	J	A	D	A
E	P	K	A	R	A	I	A	G	N	H	M	Q	R	H	F
Y	H	M	T	O	R	O	S	E	M	D	B	L	D	S	T
M	K	A	E	P	E	U	S	S	S	R	D	C	Q	O	P
K	E	H	U	H	N	S	P	T	O	C	C	U	P	Y	N
P	Z	D	R	E	T	H	P	N	W	K	B	N	G	R	L
B	N	O	T	T	F	A	M	I	L	I	A	R	A	J	B

Fact v Opinion Level 1 Quiz 4

Match the statements to the matching FACT or OPINION image

1. Marge Simpson's maiden name is Bouvier

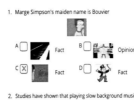

A ☐ Fact   B ☐ Opinion
C ☒ Fact   D ☐ Fact

2. Studies have shown that playing slow background music can make you eat food at a slower rate.

A ☐ Fact   B ☒ Fact
C ☐ Fact   D ☐ Fact

3. Manchester United are a much better football team than Chelsea.

A ☐ Opinion   B ☒ Opinion
C ☐ Opinion   D ☐ Opinion

4. Elton John's single, Candle in the Wind (Princess Diana tribute version) sold over 37 million copies worldwide, making it one of the best-selling songs of all time.

A ☐ Opinion   B ☐ Fact
C ☐ Fact   D ☒ Fact

5. Dogs make better pets than cats.

A ☐ Fact   B ☒ Opinion
C ☐ Opinion   D ☐ Fact

6. It is ethically unacceptable to inflict suffering on one species in the hope of trying to help another.

A ☐ Fact   B ☒ Opinion
C ☐ Fact   D ☐ Opinion

7. Since its introduction in February 1935, more than 200 million Monopoly board games have been sold worldwide.

A ☒ Fact   B ☐ Fact
C ☐ Opinion   D ☐ Opinion

8. The intimidation and violent actions of anti-vivisection protesters are deplorable.

A ☐ Opinion   B ☐ Fact
C ☐ Opinion   D ☒ Opinion

Spelling Level 1 Quiz 2

Rearrange these letters to spell out the correct words.

1. p i i n a r c p l
   p r i n c i p a l

2. p i i n l r c p e
   p r i n c i p l e

3. e a r p p a n t
   a p p a r e n t

4. c p u y o c
   o c c u p y

5. a r f t d
   d r a f t

6. a d r t h u g
   d r a u g h t

7. o p r t e p h
   p r o p h e t

8. o i f t p r
   p r o f i t

9. f e e t
   f e e t

10. f a e t
    f e a t

11. i i l a m f a r
    f a m i l i a r

12. a e r d h
    h e a r d

13. h r e d
    h e r d

14. a a m r u t e
    a m a t e u r

15. e t w h t l f
    t w e l f t h

16. c a h t y
    y a c h t

17. a l t r i a p c r u
    p a r t i c u l a r

18. o n i s u o c c s
    c o n s c i o u s

19. a b r a s m r e s
    e m b a r r a s s

20. g s u t s g e
    s u g g e s t

Spelling Level 1 Quiz 3

Find the 20 words. They can be found up, down, across or diagonal.

1. either	2. neither	3. protein	4. seize	5. precede
6. proceed	7. caffeine	8. applied	9. attaches	10. attached
11. tomatoes	12. restaurant	13. conscience	14. immediate	15. teamwork
16. leaves	17. deceive	18. conceive	19. ceiling	20. perceive

```
R K A V X G V C J M Y B A A P B Y
E C D M C P S A E H T W V T R A R
S E R N O E F F Y U O S V T O F C
T I C L N R F F Y S M V A A T B U
A L I M C C X E L X A W D C E C X
U I E J E E R I E V T E N H I O T
R N A A I I S N A I O D J E N N A
A G T X V V P E V W E F N S L S N
N I E S E E R F E P S P O J E C V
T M A E P A O K S U V G T W T I U
Y M M I R P C C S L A Y V E Q E B
M E W Z E P E B N E I T H E R N D
W D O E C L E D E C E I V E I C W
Q I R A E I D L A Q L Y S W V E L
G A K O D E Y P A T T A C H E D E
K T D X E D J Z O W O W I M G Q K
D E E I T H E R H D S S S K C W B
```

Spelling Level 1 Quiz 4

Rearrange these letters to spell out the correct words.

1. e i t r h e
   `e i t h e r`
2. t r e e h n i
   `n e i t h e r`
3. t n i r e p o
   `p r o t e i n`
4. e z e i s
   `s e i z e`
5. c e d r e p e
   `p r e c e d e`
6. c d e r e p o
   `p r o c e e d`
7. f f i e e a n c
   `c a f f e i n e`
8. l d e p i a p
   `a p p l i e d`
9. t a h s c t e a
   `a t t a c h e s`
10. t a h d c t e a
    `a t t a c h e d`
11. m a o s t o e t
    `t o m a t o e s`
12. t s r e r t a a n u
    `r e s t a u r a n t`
13. e n c o e s n c c i
    `c o n s c i e n c e`
14. i e m d t a e i m
    `i m m e d i a t e`
15. a m o k w e r t
    `t e a m w o r k`
16. l e a s v e
    `l e a v e s`
17. e e v e i d c
    `d e c e i v e`
18. n c i e e o v c
    `c o n c e i v e`
19. l g n e i c i
    `c e i l i n g`
20. r c i e e e v p
    `p e r c e i v e`

Spelling Level 1 Quiz 5

Find the 20 words. They can be found up, down, across or diagonal.

1. ought	2. nought	3. fought	4. thought	5. borough
6. bridle	7. bridal	8. cemetery	9. rhyme	10. disastrous
11. foreign	12. relevant	13. individual	14. necessary	15. muscle
16. stomach	17. cities	18. knives	19. buses	20. brushes

```
C T H O U G H T L E C K D K F A
M U S C L E N C P G M P I P M C
N E C E S S A R Y P Y D S C O E
W M P F O U G H T K B Q A S C M
I C R B R I D A L F R A S L F E
X I H R U V F Q X Z U B T L O T
Z N Y D H M L W Q I S O R J R E
W D M K N I V E S Z H L O B E R
J I E B R I D L E T E K U O I Y
T V U G W L C M L K S H S R G A
A I C G C I T I E S G E G O N Y
B D U X R E L E V A N T N U Z H
U U H O U G H T A B E Y H G H T
S A N F D P T J D E H F K H H C
E L X Y Z W Y F H N O U G H T P
S L S K M H H X E S T O M A C H
```

Spelling Level 1 Quiz 6

Rearrange these letters to spell out the correct words.

1. t h o u g
   `o u g h t`
2. n g t o h u
   `n o u g h t`
3. f g t o h u
   `f o u g h t`
4. h t h u g t o
   `t h o u g h t`
5. g b o o u h r
   `b o r o u g h`
6. b d e r l i
   `b r i d l e`
7. b d l r a i
   `b r i d a l`
8. e e c r m e t y
   `c e m e t e r y`
9. e m r h y
   `r h y m e`
10. s r d u o s t s a i
    `d i s a s t r o u s`
11. g f o e i n r
    `f o r e i g n`
12. e a r n l e v t
    `r e l e v a n t`
13. l d i a u d i v i n
    `i n d i v i d u a l`
14. s n y e s r e c a
    `n e c e s s a r y`
15. m c e u l s
    `m u s c l e`
16. c s t m a h o
    `s t o m a c h`
17. c i s i e t
    `c i t i e s`
18. k v s n e i
    `k n i v e s`
19. s e b u s
    `b u s e s`
20. e b r s h s u
    `b r u s h e s`

Spelling Level 1 Quiz 7

Find the 20 words. They can be found up, down, across or diagonal.

1. existence
2. lightning
3. interrupt
4. devise
5. device
6. awkward
7. assent
8. bored
9. board
10. mourning
11. morning
12. according
13. ascent
14. cereal
15. serial
16. symbol
17. complement
18. compliment
19. complete
20. bruise

```
I G W O I T W L M X C X Q E C A X
K N F L F H L K J X L I E I Q C I
H R T C O M P L E T E D W T H C B
B C A E Z H I R N C U H M B V O V
R O Q W R S L I G H T N I N G R A
U M E Y K R S Y M B O L E Q R D B
I P D X O W U M O R N I N G R I O
S L M E I O A P Z F R O H G R N A
E I A A V S B R T X N Z N N D A N
B M S V L I T L D N Q I F H E I D
W E S E K S S E H N N H E Y L C R
E N E R W E A E N R I C V A Q X D
F T N R A D R S U C I W I K W E W
G W T Q Q X V O C V E R N G R N V
Y N Y S A T M X E E E D Z O I H K
C E R E A L Z D C S N F B B V A G
E C O M P L E M E N T T X O L Y S
```

Spelling Level 1 Quiz 8

Rearrange these letters to spell out the correct words.

1. n e x c e t s i e
   `e x i s t e n c e`
2. i g i n n t h g l
   `l i g h t n i n g`
3. u t n p r r e t i
   `i n t e r r u p t`
4. e v i d s e
   `d e v i s e`
5. e v i d c e
   `d e v i c e`
6. a d w r k w a
   `a w k w a r d`
7. t s e a n s
   `a s s e n t`
8. o b d e r
   `b o r e d`
9. o b d r a
   `b o a r d`
10. o u r i n g n m
    `m o u r n i n g`
11. m g n n r o i
    `m o r n i n g`
12. i g c n d r o c a
    `a c c o r d i n g`
13. t c e a n s
    `a s c e n t`
14. l r e c a e
    `c e r e a l`
15. l r i s a e
    `s e r i a l`
16. l m b s o y
    `s y m b o l`
17. t o l e p n m e m c
    `c o m p l e m e n t`
18. t o l e p n m i m c
    `c o m p l i m e n t`
19. o m p e t e l c
    `c o m p l e t e`
20. e u i b s r
    `b r u i s e`

Spelling Level 1 Quiz 9

Find the 20 words. They can be found up, down, across or diagonal.

1. loose
2. lose
3. stationary
4. stationery
5. ancient
6. neighbour
7. everyday
8. wary
9. weary
10. nuisance
11. calves
12. temperature
13. parties
14. liquid
15. quest
16. queue
17. quick
18. quill
19. sincere
20. variety

```
D J F N U I S A N C E E T Y W K
U N W J S V P L L U Q Q U I C K
B B T S P E V E R Y D A Y Y V I
T I E E H L L K T S S P R Z G D
E W E A R Y W N E E Q A Z V Q D
M F G I S S E U R U N P G M I A
P W S G Q I T K X O L U T U S C
E L V J C Y X A I Q G C Q C E H
R A H N G N M T T T C I Y S W E
A A A V R R A P S I L A O G R O
T Q G A L T L E A O O L L E S L
U U G R S X U O O R O N C V L I
R E I I D Q A V O P T N E I E F
E U N E I Q T F Y S I I U R W S
H E Q T W A R Y J S E Q E O Y N
L Q C Y N E I G H B O U R S B A
```

Spelling Level 1 Quiz 10

Rearrange these letters to spell out the correct words.

1. e o s o l
   `l o o s e`
2. o i s e
   `l o s e`
3. s t n o r a y i a t
   `s t a t i o n a r y`
4. s t n o r e y i a t
   `s t a t i o n e r y`
5. i n a n t c e
   `a n c i e n t`
6. e b o u g i r n h
   `n e i g h b o u r`
7. r e y e a v y d
   `e v e r y d a y`
8. a w r y
   `w a r y`
9. y a r e w
   `w e a r y`
10. s n a i c u e n
    `n u i s a n c e`
11. a s v l c e
    `c a l v e s`
12. t r e e u t a r m p e
    `t e m p e r a t u r e`
13. t e p a s r i
    `p a r t i e s`
14. i d u q l i
    `l i q u i d`
15. t e s u q
    `q u e s t`
16. e e u u q
    `q u e u e`
17. k i c u q
    `q u i c k`
18. l i l u q
    `q u i l l`
19. c r s i e n e
    `s i n c e r e`
20. i t v a y r e
    `v a r i e t y`

Spelling Level 1 Quiz 11

Find the 20 words. They can be found up, down, across or diagonal.

1. leisure	2. programme	3. language	4. alter	5. altar
6. interfere	7. vegetable	8. profession	9. affects	10. effects
11. persuade	12. appearance	13. specific	14. official	15. pension
16. verified	17. secretary	18. equipped	19. attempt	20. reception

```
B V Q M P E R S U A D E C I J T X
W G P L E I S U R E I R R E P W V
D T A H N X F W I N T E R F E R E
E O T P E Q U I P P E D M A J O E
Z S T G V E G E T A B L E L V B W
V P E R E C E P T I O N W T Y M S
E E M P R O F E S S I O N E J U P
R C P O F F I C I A L G K R C U
I I T K A S D Q V U J R E O P H X
F F K P F A W W C C X H N S E A B
I I U R F P R O G R A M M E N M G
E C O Y E L A N G U A G E P S E C
D I L Z C H O E F F E C T S I W W
N I G D T D U A L T A R Z I O O B
T X F J S L R S X D O H X E N U O
O F M E T C H S E C R E T A R Y Z
B X E I A P P E A R A N C E R C H
```

Spelling Level 1 Quiz 12

Date: _____

Rearrange these letters to spell out the correct words.

1. i e s u r l e
   `l e i s u r e`
2. m r p r m g o e a
   `p r o g r a m m e`
3. n u g g a e l a
   `l a n g u a g e`
4. l a e t r
   `a l t e r`
5. l a a t r
   `a l t a r`
6. r n i r e e t e f
   `i n t e r f e r e`
7. l e v t b e g e a
   `v e g e t a b l e`
8. e i n p o f o s r s
   `p r o f e s s i o n`
9. f s e c t a f
   `a f f e c t s`
10. f s e c t e f
    `e f f e c t s`
11. r u d s e e p a
    `p e r s u a d e`

12. a n e a p e c a p r
    `a p p e a r a n c e`
13. e i i c p c s f
    `s p e c i f i c`
14. f c a i f l o i
    `o f f i c i a l`
15. n n s i o p e
    `p e n s i o n`
16. r f e i e d v i
    `v e r i f i e d`
17. r e s e a r c y t
    `s e c r e t a r y`
18. u p e i q d e p
    `e q u i p p e d`
19. t t e m p a t
    `a t t e m p t`
20. o e r p i e c n t
    `r e c e p t i o n`

Spelling Level 1 Quiz 13

Find the 20 words. They can be found up, down, across or diagonal.

1. achieve	2. vehicle	3. equipped	4. business	5. industry
6. temporary	7. hygiene	8. awareness	9. experience	10. security
11. progress	12. receive	13. recognise	14. identify	15. career
16. evidence	17. equipment	18. function	19. physical	20. structure

```
W P H Y S I C A L C V U F A P N Y U I
B D V E H I C L E H H M U W R M X U E
L E X P E R I E N C E L N A O S Q P I
S T E M P O R A R Y B M C R G E Y R A
L N C Q B O M K C U M B T E R S K C K
R I G D K M C B D S V V I N E M E Q A
B I D E R V G E U W T I O E S H T B R
N A N E M E A F I S T R N S S U X G A
H C C D N G C Q R Q I A U S I P D B E
S H U A U T S O P K Y N W C V T E G Q
I I W N R S I X G K T A E V T N Y B U
Z E B J N E T F Z N K E U S E U F L I
V V T E O X E R Y R I J I I S S R Q P
P E O D W E E R Y E Y S G O S C V E M
C U Y J C T G A D C J Y E N P U E X E
S G S B L B S S M E H W E X H A B T N
E Q U I P P E D U I O W T O E X U M T
C T O C W B T H P V S E C U R I T Y Z
V F Q T G Z O D S E E V I D E N C E S
```

Spelling Level 1 Quiz 14

Rearrange these letters to spell out the correct words.

1. e h i a v e c
   `a c h i e v e`
2. e h i v l c e
   `v e h i c l e`
3. p u e i p q d e
   `e q u i p p e d`
4. e s b i n u s s
   `b u s i n e s s`
5. t d i u s n y r
   `i n d u s t r y`
6. m r e r y t p a o
   `t e m p o r a r y`
7. e g i h n e y
   `h y g i e n e`
8. a s w n s a r e e
   `a w a r e n e s s`
9. e i r e e c x p e n
   `e x p e r i e n c e`
10. i c s u r e y t
    `s e c u r i t y`
11. e o p g r r s s
    `p r o g r e s s`

12. e c e r v i e
    `r e c e i v e`
13. c s e n e r o i g
    `r e c o g n i s e`
14. i e i n t d y f
    `i d e n t i f y`
15. e c e a r r
    `c a r e e r`
16. n i e d e v e c
    `e v i d e n c e`
17. u n q m t e i e p
    `e q u i p m e n t`
18. i n f c t u n o
    `f u n c t i o n`
19. c y p s i h l a
    `p h y s i c a l`
20. r r t t e s u u c
    `s t r u c t u r e`

86

Spelling Level 1 Quiz 15

Find the 20 words. They can be found up, down, across or diagonal.

1. maintained	2. department	3. workload	4. advise	5. quality
6. research	7. community	8. challenge	9. question	10. soldier
11. evaluate	12. strategy	13. consumer	14. exchange	15. explain
16. survey	17. nominate	18. studio	19. ethics	20. developing

```
C  C  P  N  J  K  D  E  X  P  L  A  I  N  B  M  W
H  O  Z  K  R  V  B  B  P  X  L  E  T  H  I  C  S
A  N  Y  E  X  C  H  A  N  G  E  Y  O  I  E  T  A
L  S  W  P  S  N  I  P  C  W  O  R  K  L  O  A  D
L  U  M  S  U  R  V  E  Y  N  Q  K  Q  R  D  H  V
E  M  I  T  M  X  Z  E  V  A  L  U  A  T  E  H  V
N  E  J  W  A  I  E  H  L  S  T  U  D  I  O  S  Q
G  R  M  G  D  E  P  A  R  T  M  E  N  T  Z  T  U
E  J  L  K  T  S  C  O  M  M  U  N  I  T  Y  R  A
U  Q  D  Y  Z  T  A  D  V  I  S  E  H  X  I  A  L
C  U  J  K  A  V  R  E  S  E  A  R  C  H  S  T  I
J  E  M  N  O  M  I  N  A  T  E  I  L  O  S  E  T
I  S  X  O  M  A  I  N  T  A  I  N  E  D  H  G  Y
U  T  S  O  L  D  I  E  R  H  G  Z  U  M  A  Y  X
G  I  U  R  L  F  S  M  T  W  Q  D  W  U  J  L  N
K  O  D  C  C  Q  P  F  I  P  X  A  U  A  K  S  F
A  N  B  E  S  Q  B  D  E  V  E  L  O  P  I  N  G
```

Spelling Level 1 Quiz 16

Rearrange these letters to spell out the correct words.

1. a d m n t a n i e i
   m a i n t a i n e d

2. t t d a r e e m n p
   d e p a r t m e n t

3. o d a r w k l o
   w o r k l o a d

4. v e d a s i
   a d v i s e

5. q u t l i y a
   q u a l i t y

6. e h c s r e a r
   r e s e a r c h

7. c m i y u o m n t
   c o m m u n i t y

8. c l n e l h a e g
   c h a l l e n g e

9. u n o e q s t i
   q u e s t i o n

10. s o e d i r l
    s o l d i e r

11. v e t a e l u a
    e v a l u a t e

12. t y g r s a t e
    s t r a t e g y

13. o r e n c s u m
    c o n s u m e r

14. x e g c e h a n
    e x c h a n g e

15. e x i l a n p
    e x p l a i n

16. r y u s e v
    s u r v e y

17. o e t m n i n a
    n o m i n a t e

18. u o t s i d
    s t u d i o

19. h s t e c i
    e t h i c s

20. o g d e l e i p n v
    d e v e l o p i n g

REMEMBER: EVERY SENTENCE STARTS WITH A CAPITAL LETTER. MAKE SURE THE EXAMINER CAN CLEARLY SEE IT IS A CAPITAL!